W9-ANF-524

TEEN VOICES
from the
HOLY LAND

TEEN VOICES
FROM THE
HOLY LAND

Who Am I to You?

Mahmoud Watad
and
Leonard Grob

Prometheus Books

59 John Glenn Drive
Amherst, New York 14228–2197

Published 2007 by Prometheus Books

Teen Voices from the Holy Land: Who Am I to You? Copyright © 2007 by Mahmoud Watad and Leonard Grob. All rights reserved. No part of this publication may be reproduced, stored in a retrieval system, or transmitted in any form or by any means, digital, electronic, mechanical, photocopying, recording, or otherwise, or conveyed via the Internet or a Web site without prior written permission of the publisher, except in the case of brief quotations embodied in critical articles and reviews.

Inquiries should be addressed to
Prometheus Books
59 John Glenn Drive
Amherst, New York 14228–2197
VOICE: 716–691–0133, ext. 207
FAX: 716–564–2711
WWW.PROMETHEUSBOOKS.COM

11 10 09 08 07   5 4 3 2 1

Library of Congress Cataloging-in-Publication Data

Watad, Mahmoud.
  Teen voices from the Holy Land : who am I to you? / Mahmoud Watad and Leonard Grob.
    p. cm.
  Includes bibliographical references.
  ISBN 978–1–59102–535–1 (alk. paper)
  1. Children—Israel—Biography—Juvenile literature. 2. Jewish children—Israel—Biography—Juvenile literature. 3. Children, Palestinian Arab—Israel—Biography—Juvenile literature. 4. Israel—Ethnic relations. I. Grob, Leonard. II. Title.

CT1919.P343W37 2007
305.892'400922—dc22
[B]   2007001565

Printed in the United States of America on acid-free paper

To the children of Palestine, Israel, and
throughout the world

who are the hope for a world of justice and peace

CONTENTS

ACKNOWLEDGMENTS

The authors would like to thank first and foremost the Palestinian and Israeli children who gave their time and shared candid descriptions of their lives and their passion for peace and justice so that this book could be written. We also thank the families of these teenagers for their support.

We wish to express our gratitude to all those who worked to make this book come to life: Irit Bloomgarden, Rotem Garinikol, Meirav Grinstein, Yifat Har-Even, Khaled Khaskia, Tal Nitsani, Abed Awad, Donna Marie Moyes, and Rafiqa Othman. Special thanks go to Mufida Abdel-Rahman both for her work as editor and for her administrative contributions to the project.

Finally, we wish to say how thankful we are to Pastora Campos Goldner, whose deep generosity allowed us to initiate and sustain the work of GOHIP, the Global Oral History Project.

INTRODUCTION

During the summer of 2004, we interviewed thirty-four Palestinian and Israeli teenagers. These teens were asked to share various aspects of their ordinary, day-to-day lives and their dreams for the future. We chose to interview young people between the ages of twelve and eighteen, as we strongly believe this is an age group that can make a difference in the world. The teenagers whose stories you are about to read are ingenuous and candid, bringing spontaneity, openness, and sincerity to the stories they tell. They are willing to speak their mind. Their stories consist of jovial, plaintive, and heartrending testimonies. Our aim is to provide you with a window into the soul of each child, to find the hope that lies in the innocence of youth.

The Palestinian-Israeli conflict has occupied a central place on the world stage for nearly a century. It has served as a source of great pain to the peoples of the region, and the resultant agony has impacted the rest of the world. Even after a political solution has been reached, it may still be a matter of generations before demonization of the "other"—Israeli or Palestinian—is replaced by an ongoing process of humanization. We hope this book will promote greater understanding between Israelis and Palestinians, furthering the process of humanizing the "other." Our hope is for the narratives to spark reflections about the value of commonalities and an appreciation of differences among peoples within our own borders in the United States and across the globe.

Teen Voices from the Holy Land: Who Am I to You? offers a kaleidoscope of verbal and pictorial snapshots of children's lives. Through the voices of children who live in the Middle East, we hope that the reader will enter their lives and gain a deeper understanding of what is occurring in this part of the world. We are confident that these narratives will provide food for thought regarding how people anywhere in the world might take a more active role in promoting the values of peace and mutual understanding embraced by the children in this book.

Many of the children interviewed admit that they have had minimal or no contact with children on "the other side." Most Palestinians have had little contact with Israelis other than with soldiers at checkpoints or with security personnel at airports. Many Israeli teenagers encounter Palestinians only at chance meetings. We hope this book will help introduce the youth of each people to one another, dispelling harmful stereotypes along the way. Additionally, we hope that the reader, while getting to know each teen through his or her portrait, will appreciate the deep humanity residing within each child.

To share a variety of aspects of these children's experiences, we organized the interviews around the following categories: (1) Family Histories and Dynamics; (2) Lives in the Schoolroom; (3) Lives in the Neighborhood; (4) Friendships; (5) Personal Hobbies and Interests; (6) Religious and Spiritual Concerns; (7) Cultural Dynamics; (8) Political Concerns; and (9) Dreams for the Future. Most of the narratives begin with biographical details: the age of the child, where she lives, and her family. Each child was encouraged to speak freely; some focused more on family issues, whereas others spoke in greater detail about school. Some emphasized the friendships in their lives while others talked more freely about their dreams for the future.

In an effort to whet your appetite to read on, we have included some relevant quotations from the children regarding each of the above-mentioned categories.

FAMILY HISTORIES

The reader will find that most of the teenagers are quite open about family matters. Times of intimacy and times of dissension are described, sometimes with poignancy, often with brutal honesty. Yuval's mother is described as "everyone's mom." "When people sleep at my home and wake up in the morning," Yuval says, "they say, 'Good morning, Mom.'" Jad says, "I can't remember an unhappy moment in my family." Khael gives an example of the kind of freedom his father gives him to make his own decisions: "Once I told him that I wanted to become a priest. My father didn't interfere. He just warned me not to make such a decision too quickly." Tal tells of a time when her mother refused to buy a pair of pants for her: "I screamed at her and told her she was a bad mother and that I would not talk with her for the rest of my life. But not-talking-to-my-mom lasted only an hour."

Sibling rivalries are a frequent subject of discussion. Haneen says that "[w]hen it comes to doing work at home, my parents know that I'm the oldest and that I should do more of the work. But when they give presents, they forget that I'm the one with all the responsibilities." Murad echoes this point when he recounts how much responsibility falls to him as the eldest of four children: "[I]t seems that in a family the eldest brother is oppressed." Shir speaks of fighting "about everything" with her brothers. Nofar describes aspects of her relationship with her sister as follows: "I don't listen to a lot of music, and she does. When she puts on music, I scream. She's more involved with her studies, while I'm more interested in socializing."

Some speak of the effect of divorce or the death of a parent on their lives. Ella's dream for the future is simply put: "I would want my mother and father to be together again." Sandy calls her late mother her "ideal person," someone who "could do anything," a woman with a "sixth sense about things." Others recount times when parents helped them resolve seemingly irresolvable conflicts with friends or teachers. Yuval says he made it through eleventh grade "thanks to Mom. She just did not let me rest. She sat on me for a month." Maor tells us that he appreciates his father because "I tell him my secrets, and he doesn't reveal them to anyone, even my mother." Humor often enters into tales about family life. Abdullah, age thirteen, describes a burn on his leg incurred, accidentally, during an act of mischief. When asked by his mother why he didn't tell her of the burn before visiting the village clinic, Abdullah replies, "Burning is less severe than your tongue."

LIVES IN THE SCHOOLROOM

The teenagers address in-depth their day-to-day lives as middle school and high school students. Some express feelings of boredom in the classroom and talk of strategies they employ to cope with such feelings. Sireen tries to distract her teachers from the subject matter under discussion: "I ask lots of questions...that sometimes are not that relevant. For example, I'll ask my teacher about her vacation. Then she'll forget about the subject we're studying." Others decry the lack of respect they perceive on the part of their teachers: "I hated the third grade most of all," Abdullah exclaims, "because my teacher made fun of me when I tried to read and spell Hebrew words." Afkar complains about a lack of creativity on the part of her teachers. "[They] don't encourage us to be original in our thinking. They're only interested in finishing the book and having us take exams." Tamara complains that "[s]ometimes what a teacher demands is unreasonable. For example, a teacher may say, 'Sit in your place and be quiet, you're coming to school for your own good.'" "But," Tamara concludes, "I know what's good for me."

Many teenagers sing the praises of their teachers and of their daily lives at school. The same Abdullah who was critical of his third-grade teacher pays tribute to a second-grade instructor who "recognized the fact that some students need help" and who gave him extra lessons. For Maor, "[a]n excellent teacher...is one who...has faith in you, even when you're not so successful in your studies." Tamara tells us that "teachers can affect generations to come" and she recalls the Muslim saying "The teacher was about to be a prophet." Matan attends an "open school," a school where "you can choose what you're going to study and the methods you'll be using to learn the subjects you've chosen. You're personally involved in everything that happens at the school." He goes on to add, "I'm just not interested in having someone limit my range of possibilities."

LIVES IN THE NEIGHBORHOOD

Neighborhood life is vividly described by these young Israelis and Palestinians. Most speak of close ties among neighbors. Tamara says, "We have eight houses on our block. I feel they're one house.... When we visit a relative, we just knock on the door and go in." Haneen says, "Most of our neighbors are our relatives. They're my grandparents, uncles, and cousins." Shany speaks of a neighbor who "drops in if she's passing by," and praises her mother who, busy as she is in her law firm, "makes sure she has time for these kinds of visits."

The inner life of the children interviewed cannot be separated from the political context in which they live. Thus, while describing their neighborhoods, many Palestinian teenagers complain bitterly about Israeli checkpoints preventing them from moving about within and between their immediate surroundings. As Sireen says, "When you want to visit another place, you have to think about it a thousand times, because in order to leave the neighborhood, you have to wait an hour and a half just to go through the checkpoint." According to Khael, "Before the Occupation a trip from Birzeit to Ramallah, where I go to school, would be an easy, lovely ride. But now it's not the case. Yesterday a barrier was erected, and we were late to school."

The ongoing conflict means that crossing neighborhood boundaries—or even moving about within a neighborhood—is stressful for Israelis in a different way. Many Israeli teenagers speak of their fear of suicide bombs, a fear that prevents them from moving freely outside their homes. "Once," Asaf says, "I rode a bus and saw a Palestinian get onto the bus with some bags. I felt afraid, so I got off one stop early."

Daniel says, "Our region is not a fun place to be. If you want to go to the seashore, you're afraid that a suicide bomber will come up from the water."

The inextricable linkage between inner and outer lives becomes even more apparent when many Palestinian interviewees—discussing life in their neighborhoods—complain about the lack of funds for Palestinian Israeli communities compared with the availability of funds for Jewish Israeli neighborhood facilities. Reem decries the fact that "[o]ur village doesn't have playgrounds or parks. There's just no money in our municipal budget for parks. We have to go to the Jewish towns if we want to play in places like these." Alaa claims that "[a] lack of funds in the Palestinian community is the main cause of the suffering that's occurring in Palestinian cities within Israel." Jad dreams of being a professional basketball player, but, in his words, "I don't have access to decent facilities and coaches.... The kibbutzim [collective communities] and Jewish towns surrounding [my town] all have very beautiful, modern sports facilities, but I can't go there to practice." Sandy is an excellent swimmer. When thinking about trying out for the Olympics, she realizes that there are many stumbling blocks for Palestinians. She cannot practice her swimming in Olympic-sized facilities: "My identity card doesn't permit me to go in and out of Jerusalem."

FRIENDSHIPS

Descriptions of friendships make up substantial portions of each teenager's narrative. Yuval says, "[My friends] don't let me be sad. When I'm really depressed, they just don't allow me to stay that way." Khael's four close friends confide in one another. "Sometimes there are misunderstandings among us, but we forgive each other pretty quickly. Friendship is a treasure that can be yours for life." Elinor's friends are "like sisters." For Reem, "[f]riendship...is like living in a steady stream of sincerity, honesty, love, and cooperation flowing from one person to another." Some teenagers talk about difficulties in making and sustaining friendships. Hala has trouble expressing her feelings to her friends: "I just can't talk to them. I keep it all inside, and it continues to hurt." Nofar confesses that she does not get along with boys. "They only bother me." And Alaa proclaims, "Friendship isn't always smooth." She gives an example replete with irony: "We agreed to go out together to the mall to see a movie. It turned out that there wasn't enough room in the car for all of us, so I volunteered to stay home. My friend simply accepted what I had offered to do.... I was angry and felt that she was being very selfish."

Friendships with members of the opposite sex are also discussed. Most Palestinians mention that their cultural traditions prohibit them from forming more than casual friendships with members of the opposite sex prior to marriage. Ahmad says, "I... like spending time with a group of girls. However, the society I live in does not encourage this practice. I feel envious when I see Israeli teenagers relating to their female friends." Sireen's testimony on this subject is striking: "My parents forbid me from having a boyfriend because of our tradition. I think having male friends is OK, but it would be silly to have a boyfriend. I have friends who have boyfriends. One day, one of them told me, 'We had fun,' and then the following day she said, 'We broke up.'... If you have a fight with a male friend, you'll get over it in two or three days. But a fight with a boyfriend would break your heart."

A few of the older Israeli teenagers speak quite candidly about boyfriend-girlfriend relationships. For Nadia, "The important thing in a relationship like mine with my boyfriend is honesty. We should have a good time and not be pressured to do anything we don't want to do." Yuval speaks of the end of a relationship: "There was someone I fell in love with not long ago. I asked her if she wanted to move ahead with our relationship. She said she didn't know, that she needed to think about it. She thought about it for a really long time. That really upset me.... There's a limit to waiting for love." An important part of Shany's inner life is revealed when she tells us, "My dreams for the future include finding someone who will love me and whom I'll love in return. But first of all I've got to be OK within myself."

PERSONAL HOBBIES AND INTERESTS

All of the teenagers speak of their passion for hobbies or interests outside of school. Often these descriptions of extracurricular activities shed light on the inner life of the interviewee. Nofar reveals that she is very interested in art and that she draws nicely. However, she is unsure of herself: "My father says I have a very successful future in art. He tells everyone that his daughter will be an artist someday. But I feel insecure about my drawing. Maybe I don't appreciate myself enough." Nadia admits that she excels in analyzing other people. After offering an astute interpretation of a dream, she is asked by her mother, "How do you know all this?" Nadia's reply: "I just knew it. I sort of felt it. I don't know where I got this ability from." Abdullah spent time with a cat that he loved. Yet after giving the cat all his attention for a long time, Abdullah tells us, "I got busy with other things, and I stopped feeding it. The cat slipped away quietly." He concludes, "I guess every creature wants to be cared for all the time."

Ibraheem practices karate, earning a brown belt and working toward a black belt. "What I love about karate," he tells us, "is the discipline. This is the same discipline I get from practicing my faith." Tal loves acting: "I'd like to be an actress someday," she proclaims. "I'll first want to be successful in Israel, then on to Hollywood. What I especially like about acting is the possibility of achieving fame and becoming rich. I want everyone to know who Tal is." Sari is entranced by the music of the Colombian singer Shakira: "Shakira's sweet songs connect me to God," he shares. "They nourish my soul." Uri speaks of letting go of his anger by sitting down and drawing: "I love drawing," he says. "It helps me forget my problems." Humor is not lacking in this category either. Daniel, who lives with his mother, describes his piano lessons as a failed experiment: "My mother has always wanted me to be a pianist. She actually forced me to study piano.... You can bet the neighbors are pleased when I practice the piano at my father's home!"

RELIGIOUS AND SPIRITUAL CONCERNS

Almost every one of the teenagers has something to say about his or her religious/spiritual life. Sireen says, "Our prophet taught us what we should and shouldn't do. Regardless of our mistakes, if we ask God to forgive us, God will do so.... Fear of punishment prevents you from repeating bad things." Shirli says, "I feel close to God when I see...the little things people do." Reem stresses the difference between a belief in God rooted in fear and a belief grounded in love. Quoting the Prophet Muhammad, Reem says, "I follow the principles of Islam just because I love Allah, not because I fear him." Ayelet is linked to her Jewish tradition through her sense of community gained by observing the rules of Judaism: "[W]hat connects [Jews] to one another is our religion," she says. Afkar declares, "[A Muslim] has to tell the truth and care for others' possessions the way he cares for his own." Yuval says, "I think there is a superior being who created us the way we are." Many children stress their tradition's call to respect everyone: "Islam," Haneen says, "asks us to behave with integrity and to love people without considering their color, race, or religion. It's enough that he's a human being." Uri declares, "We all believe in the same God." Sandy proclaims that "God lives in the soul of every one of us."

Some teenagers express doubts regarding strict adherence to traditional belief systems. Daniel questions God's goodness and justice, alluding to the Holocaust and other instances of evil in our world. "Where is God?" he asks. "There was a war from 1939 until 1945. And where is God now? With the Palestinians? With the Israelis? If there hadn't been a Holocaust, my belief in God would be stronger. I would be prepared not to travel on the Sabbath." Although a believer, Alaa questions some aspects of the way her religion is practiced by some of its adherents: "I believe in God, even though I don't pray on a regular basis. But I do fast during the month of Ramadan....But I certainly don't like the fact that very religious people try to interfere with our daily lives. For example, my grandfather pesters me all the time not to do this and not to do that." Shany is bothered by the existence of present-day evils: "I have to say that if God exists, I hope he doesn't live in any one place. I hope he travels around the world all the time. If there's a God, there are lots of things he needs to do in our world."

CULTURAL DYNAMICS

Examples of adherence to—or questions about—cultural norms abound in every narrative. Although matters relating to culture permeate each aspect of the children's word portraits, elements of allegiance to or alienation from cultural traditions warrant special note. Haneen loves traditional weddings: "When a bride and groom are happy, it seems as if the entire world shares their joy. When I get married," she proclaims, "my wedding will follow the traditional customs." Yet Haneen is critical of cultural biases: "Having no equality between girls and boys is unfair," she says. Ahmad is critical of the practice of inviting everyone in his village to a wedding: "When I marry, I'll arrange a simple wedding. I'll try to invite fewer people than is the norm. But I need to be realistic. In the end my father will do the inviting, and there's a custom that does not allow anyone to be excluded from the celebration." Tamara tells us that her culture encourages her to be of help to others: "Recently," she recalls, "I met a woman holding a baby who asked me to go shopping for her. I did it without hesitation. ...And if I see small children fighting, I immediately step in and stop them." For Uri the custom of sharing a Sabbath meal is of great importance because it is the only time the family can eat together and "talk about all that's happened to you during the past week."

Elinor speaks about the realization of a commonality with Palestinians of her age. Describing a meeting with Palestinian teenagers in a local mall, she exclaims: "We really connected. I realized that they're really like us." Yuval notes that in conversations with Palestinians his age, "[i]t was really nice. It was not about cursing or trying to kill each another. We sat together, laughed, and listened to the same music. We liked the same computer games.... It's as if we're the same, and all the time everyone says we're different. Where's the difference?" Hala adds that "[a] human being is a human being. There is no need to know that this one is a Muslim and that one a Christian—as if this one were black and this one white."

POLITICAL CONCERNS

With regard to political concerns, the majority of Israeli and Palestinian interviewees share a common vision of peaceful coexistence. Sireen expresses willingness to share the land: "It's the only way to solve the problems between Palestinians and Israelis.... No matter how hard it is to share the land, in the end sharing is the best solution." Ahmad emphasizes the need for a peace process: "I'm ready to share the land with people I don't like." Khael says, "We need to live with each other without problems and without some being masters and some servants." Nadia acknowledges that the Palestinian struggle for statehood resembles the struggle of Israelis to establish a state for themselves: "The Palestinians demand a homeland. They want a place to live. We were also that way once.... Israelis must talk to Palestinians and find out what they want.... It seems preferable to me now to live in a land together with the Palestinians." Shany says, "I'm ready to divide the land into Israel and Palestine so that there can be peace." Matan declares that "[w]hat's going on inside me does not have to do with whether or not I like Arabs. I see that people are living under Occupation, so I feel I have to help them." Tal would like to make peace by understanding the role that emotions play in the negotiating process.

Both Palestinians and Israelis place some blame for the current situation on their leadership. Jad contends that "Palestinians need wise leaders who have the ability and the competence to negotiate with Israel." Reem says, "The Palestinian people are dying, and the leadership hasn't done anything to help the situation." Asaf is critical of policies that have led to the Israeli Occupation of Palestinian lands on the West Bank and Gaza: "Why do we have to fight about this section of land or that one?...I'd give the Territories back to the Palestinians in exchange for peace that would be of equal value." For Maor, the settlement policies of the Israeli government are flawed: "The settlers feel that where they're living is *their* place, but in order to have peace, you have to give up something. I believe we have to give up the Territories, even though it hurts a lot to do that." Ravid adds her observation that under Occupation, the Palestinians "don't have a life....Their house is not a home."

Several teenagers emphasize the need to take some responsibility for the conduct of affairs in their region. For Shirli, people on the ground should accept responsibility for the violence in this region of the world: "The leaders play with the world as if it were a toy....I think peace starts from the people." Ahmad says that "Palestinians should unite and work closely with one another." Yuval proclaims, "It's not just the responsibility of the heads of the government. A whole nation has to arrive at a decision to make peace."

The teenagers offer multiple views of the effects of the current political situation on their daily lives. Sireen addresses the travel restrictions imposed on Palestinians by the Israeli government: "I'd like to switch places with birds. Birds have wings and can go wherever they want....I'd like to be free....But I don't feel free inside....My dream is to design a flying car, because at least it would not have to stop at checkpoints." Khael says, "Israeli soldiers don't treat me as a human being.... I hope that Israelis understand how much Palestinians suffer from the Occupation.'" Rolla claims that she's bored when she happens to be home even a few days in a row. "What about those Palestinians who can't move from one city to another for weeks, months, years at a time?" she asks. Other Palestinian teenagers place the responsibility for the situation squarely upon the shoulders of the current Israeli prime minister. Sandy asks how the prime minister's "conscience permits him to sleep, since he's responsible for the killing of innocent children." Murad says that the Israeli government "is building a very high wall to separate people from one another."

Israeli teenagers speak of their own brand of pain. Several address the necessity for peace so that they can move about free of fear of suicide bombings. Maor says, "I want to stop being fearful. I want to stop looking at the front door of the bus." Shir admits that "[t]he way the situation is now, I feel fear.... I dream about a world where there would be harmony. I'd be able to go to the mall or to a coffee shop without fear."

DREAMS FOR THE FUTURE

A majority of teenagers allude to a future in which peace will reign in the region. Haneen acknowledges the fact of diversity, but asserts that "[e]ven though there are different nationalities, customs, and religions in the world, my hope is that there will be a lasting peace." For Tamara, peace means uniting disparate nations and religions: "My ultimate dream is to unite the world, removing all borders. Most wars occur because the world is divided into countries with borders. I'd cancel the names of all countries.... There would be just one flag for one world."

Others speak of their dream to help those who are needy or oppressed. Many want to build new homes for parents or new recreational facilities for those towns and villages that lack them. "I'd build a place for the youth of [my town] to gather," says Ahmad, who adds that he would also contribute money to help his parents and the poor. Still others speak about traveling abroad or leaving their native soil to settle elsewhere. Afkar dreams about living in Germany some day: "I would not want to return to Israel. Here there's no freedom. I feel there are chains around us." Many teenagers articulate a dream about becoming a professional—physician, lawyer, chemist, inventor, educator, to name a few. Nofar aspires to enter the field of medicine where she'll specialize in pediatrics. Reem says that "someday I'll teach in Tel Aviv University." Uri tells us, "Design and architecture have always appealed to me. I think I'll go for it." Some aspire to be loving parents, husbands, or wives. Ella proclaims, simply, "I want to have lots of children—maybe three or four." Others speak in a very practical sense about their future: "When I grow up," Abdullah tells us, "I want to be a mechanic because most people have cars, and cars are always breaking down."

THE ORGANIZATION OF THE TEXT

The chapters are organized alphabetically according to the first names of the children, alternating between Palestinian and Israeli narratives. We chose to present each chapter without introductory remarks to allow each narrative to stand on its own.

We think the reader will find it useful to refer to a map showing where each child lives. Therefore, in addition to a map of the region, we include a map of Israel/Palestine with the teenagers' hometowns. And, since some readers may not be familiar with the region and some of the names and terms associated with it, we include a detailed glossary.

Additionally, we provide a time line of events that have shaped a century of the Israeli-Palestinian conflict and that, consequently, have affected the lives of the teens interviewed. Since this is not a volume about the conflict as such, we have included only landmark or milestone events in the time line. For the readers who desire additional details concerning the conflict, we provide a suggested reading list.

CHAPTER 1

ABDULLAH

"I dream of building a house with two floors, one floor for me and the other for my brother."

I'm Abdullah, age twelve. I live with my parents, two brothers, and one sister. I'm the youngest in the family. I live in Abu-Ghosh, near Jerusalem, and I go to school there. I'm entering the seventh grade. My second-grade teacher was the best teacher I've ever had. She recognized the fact that some students need help, and she gave me extra lessons. But in the grades that followed, I've received no special help. I hated the third grade most of all, because my teacher made fun of me when I tried to read and spell Hebrew words. I like speaking Hebrew, but not reading or writing it. That third-grade teacher just didn't understand me. She doesn't care about weak students. She really disrespected me.

I've always tried to study hard in school, but it takes too long for me to answer the questions on an exam. One question takes me the entire time. Then the teacher comes and grabs my paper before I've had a chance to complete the exam. When I received my report card, I burned it before arriving home. If anyone asked me about the report card, I admitted what I had done, but I felt happy when I burned it. The report card embarrassed me.

It's not unusual for me to hear that I'm a weak student. It doesn't bother me too much, though, because I know I'll do better. I'll improve my reading and writing. When I return home from school, I eat dinner, play a little, and watch TV. Sometimes I watch the news on TV, but not often. When I hear about sad things—like infants being taken from their families—I feel terrible. I love little children. They're innocent. My mother's relative runs a nursery school on the first floor of our home, and my mother helps her care for the children. I enjoy watching them play together so beautifully.

One time when I came home from school, I began playing on the roof with my friends. We made a small fire so that we could heat some tea. When we were done, I began to extinguish the fire by pouring a cup of what I thought was water on it. But it was really turpentine! The flames flared up, and my leg got burned. I was afraid to tell my mother what had happened, because she had warned me many times not to go on the roof and not to play with fire. I went to the village clinic. They treated me there and then phoned my mother. When I got home, my mother was furious with me. She asked, "Why didn't you tell me that you were burned?" I told her, "Burning is less severe than your tongue." I knew she was going to let out all her anger on me.

Later on I continued to receive treatment at the local hospital. The doctor called me "Harry Potter" because, in fact, I look like him. Whenever they'd need me to help translate Hebrew words into Arabic for Palestinian patients, they'd shout, "Harry Potter, come here." I enjoyed doing this work. I served as a "go-between," helping both patients and doctors. Whenever I heard a patient cry out that he needed help, I would immediately go get a doctor.

I have three good friends. We play either in the courtyard or inside

"Once I was caring for a cat. I gave the cat all my attention for a while, but then I got busy with other things. The cat slipped away quietly. I guess every creature wants to be cared for all the time."

my house. If one of my friends or even a sibling takes something without my permission, I get angry with them. I don't get annoyed because I've lost the object. I get upset because if I wanted something of theirs, I'd always ask them first. Why don't they ask my permission?

Animals are my friends, too. I like cats and ants. I like ants because they're small creatures and active, too. Once I was caring for a cat, feeding it milk and food. I gave the cat all my attention for a while, but then I got busy with other things, and I stopped feeding it. The cat slipped away quietly. I guess every creature wants to be cared for all the time.

I'm a Muslim. I believe in God. I always thank Allah for everything. When I listen to the call for prayer, I repeat it. I fast during the month of Ramadan. It's not so difficult. My mother does the cooking, and my sister and I prepare the table ten minutes before hearing the muezzin announcing the breaking of the fast. My mother puts food on the table, and we all sit around waiting for the call. When we hear the call, we say, "God, for you I have fasted, in you I believe, on you I have depended, and from your giving I have broken my fast." Then we start eating. After that we sit and watch special Ramadan programs on TV.

I'm very happy living in Abu-Ghosh. I'd always like to live here. I dream of building a house with two floors, one floor for me and the other for my brother. And I'd like to have one son and one daughter or perhaps two sons and two daughters. If the school in our village improves, I'll send them to it. But if it doesn't improve, I'll send them to a better school somewhere else. If I were to become rich, I'd first fix up my parents' house, inside and outside. I'd also donate money to poor people.

When I grow up I want to be a mechanic because most people have cars, and cars are always breaking down. They need to be fixed constantly. I may go abroad to complete my studies in automobile mechanics.

CHAPTER 2

ASAF

"Anarchy means that there are the fewest possible rules, and I'm for that."

I'm Asaf Rosenberg. I'm almost thirteen years old, and I'll be entering eighth grade this fall. My parents are divorced. I live with my mom, my big brother, and my younger sister. My mother and I get along fine, and we often wind up compromising about household rules. When I go to visit my friends, she usually asks that I come home by seven o'clock. But if I really beg, she'll relent. Sometimes when she asks me to come home early, I just give in. But there are times when compromising doesn't work. For example, sometimes my mother punishes me by turning off the TV while I'm watching my favorite program of the week. That really annoys me. How will I ever see that program again?

When I'm with my dad, we eat our food and then go swimming in the pool. Sometimes we go for walks on the mountainside near his house. Mainly, though, we just sit at home and talk. He recently moved closer to my mom's place. I have mixed feelings about that. It's great that he's closer to me, but on the other hand, I had made lots of friends where he used to live. Now I won't get a chance to see them.

I've just come back from a trip to Paris with Mom, Grandma, my aunt, and my cousin. In Paris we had to be careful because of all the anti-Semitism. Every time we saw someone who looked like a Palestinian, we had to be quiet and not speak Hebrew. It was my mother who insisted that we had to be quiet. If I had been in control of the situation, I would have spoken as usual. Even though I enjoyed our time abroad, I missed being with my friends.

I'm not all that involved with the traditions of my people. I really do nothing except during Chanukah when we light candles, just for the fun of it. That's it. I don't have a real connection to religion. I'm studying to prepare for my bar mitzvah, but I'm basically doing it for my grandfather. For me, personally, the whole thing has no meaning. Except, of course, that it's my birthday. I certainly would not give up on having a party. Parties are wonderful. You see lots of people, and you get to share a big meal with the whole family. People say that turning thirteen means you're an adult. But some people mature at the age of six, and others mature only when they're twenty. Everyone develops at his own pace.

When I started junior high, studies got harder. There were also new teachers, new expectations, and new classmates. But it's OK. I got used to it. The trouble with school is that I really don't like any of the subjects we study. My favorite time is recess and going to the kiosk when we get out of school early. But I have lots of friends who are in the same grade with me. Some of them are not so great. They like to be in charge of everything, which really bothers me.

"If people want to make an exchange of lands, let them do it."

I wear a chain around my neck that has an "A" in it. That's a symbol of anarchy. I saw a television program once about Palestinians. Anarchy was mentioned several times. I asked my mother what it meant, and she explained it to me. Anarchy means there are the fewest possible rules, and I'm for that. Anarchy means that there is a kind of order, but one with no fixed regulations. It means that everyone can do what they want, except that they can't hurt others. If I were driving very fast, and I could see that I wouldn't hurt anybody by doing so, why shouldn't I drive that way? Personally, I'm ready for anarchy. The way I see it, no one gets hurt.

I'm not very involved in what's happening in the country. Of course, it's important when there are attacks and people die, but it usually doesn't affect me all that much. When I start to think about it, though, I remember one time when I was in school in Kfar Saba, and an attack occurred. I knew that my mother was in the area and my brother, too. I tried to contact my mom. When I realized that the telephone lines were all busy, I got scared. There's always the fear that suddenly an attack will occur right near you. Once I rode a bus and saw a Palestinian get onto the bus with some bags. I felt afraid, so I got off one stop early. But this year I've started to ride the buses, and I feel free of fear.

I'm usually not scared when I see a Palestinian. I often see poor

Palestinian women in Memorial Garden. I see them walking in the city, too. Also, there's a Palestinian girl from Taibeh in my class. She's the only Palestinian in the school. It's just "hi" and "bye" when we meet. If she were to invite me to her house in Taibeh, I think I would go. I'd be a little scared, but in the end going there wouldn't bother me. I even chose to study Arabic in school. I thought it would help me more than French, my other choice. We're surrounded by Palestinians. Even within our country there are many Palestinians. Also, Mom says that knowing Arabic can help me when I go to the army.

I usually don't think much about questions of war and peace. But if you were to ask me what peace means, I would say that it's related to the kind of things I meant when I talked about anarchy. That each person will make his own decisions and not harm other people. That everyone will live with those people he wants to live with and will not disturb any other person. If people want to make exchanges of land, then let them do it, as long as it doesn't hurt anyone. No one should be hurt because of a dispute over the Territories. I think that if the Territories had not been so important to the Palestinians, then we would have had peace a long time ago. Also, if Yigal Amir had not murdered Yitzhak Rabin, there would have been peace long ago.

I know that the conflict we're involved in with the Palestinians is about the Territories, but I just don't understand what's so important about land. Jerusalem, from my point of view, is just like every other city, a city with lots of children. Why do we have to fight about this section of the land or that one? What difference does it make? To me, it's not important whether we're in, let's say, Uganda or whether we're here. If I were told I'd have to move because Kfar Saba is to be returned to the Palestinians, it would be OK with me—as long as I received a house of equal value to the one I live in now. In the same way, I'd give the Territories back to the Palestinians in exchange for peace that would be of equal value.

I'm really not sure what I want to do in the future. I'd like to lie back on the sofa and dream of becoming a millionaire.

CHAPTER 3

AFKAR

"It's possible to have peace only if there's equality between the two parties. Israel has no incentive to treat Palestinians as equals."

My name is Afkar. I'm sixteen years old and live in Tira with my parents and three brothers. I'm a student at Tira Secondary School. My family went through tough times when we learned that my father had cancer. We were in shock, and we were deeply concerned. I was fourteen years old at that time. Now we've become more accustomed to living with my father while he's fighting cancer. I love him very much. He's a brave man.

My neighborhood is great. I especially like visiting my relatives. I like the way people are concerned about one other, sharing both their happy and their sad times. What I don't like is the unequal treatment boys and girls receive. In the future I'll treat my sons and daughters equally. I'd like to have daughters, because I myself don't have any sisters.

I spend most of my time at home. My mother sticks to a very traditional set of rules about what I can and can't do. I'm forbidden to go out with my friends, even for a walk. I can just talk with them on the telephone. By now I'm used to staying home. On the other hand, they don't put a limit on my brothers' leisure time. They come and go as they wish.

I dream about living in Germany someday. My parents will allow me to travel to Germany because one of my brothers lives there. And I would not want to return to Israel. Here there's no freedom. I feel there are chains around us. There are no chains around a woman in Germany the way there are here.

I'm studying electronics at school. In electronics, we don't have to memorize data. We just have to use our brains. I haven't been very creative at school, because the school doesn't give us much of an opportunity to be imaginative. Teachers don't encourage us to be original in our thinking. They're only interested in finishing the book and having us take exams.

I go to school because I have to. Although I get good grades, I really don't have a good feeling about school. If I were in charge of the education system, I'd change the system and motivate students to like school. I'd add sports, swimming, and music classes. I'd try to develop students' talents by offering them activities that they care about. I wouldn't just focus on verbal skills. My dream school would encourage students to use their imagination.

I've been thinking a lot about other ways to teach and learn. It's a dream of mine to help improve the technology that allows people to attend school online. People would be able to take exams online without ever having to actually travel to school. And the online technology would allow them to study in a more creative way.

I'm Muslim, but I don't consider myself religious. Islam is about loving all people, without discriminating against anyone because of the color of his skin. If a Muslim promises something, he has to fulfill that promise. He has to tell the truth and care for others' possessions the same way he cares for his own. I wish my teachers at school would practice some of the teachings of their religion. Our lives at school would then be very different.

I don't think there's any chance that there'll be peace between the Israelis and the Palestinians. The Israelis took the Palestinians' land. They're building settlements on it. They don't want to acknowledge Palestinian rights. It's possible to have peace only if there's equality between the two parties. Israel has no incentive to treat Palestinians as equals.

CHAPTER 4

AYELET

"Usually my room is chaotic,
and when my parents
see what it looks like,
they get irritated.
They say,
'Straighten up, straighten up,'
and I reply,
'Tomorrow, tomorrow.'"

My name is Ayelet Hochman. I'm a fifteen-year-old girl living in Herzelia, and I'm one of five children in my family. I'll be entering tenth grade during the coming year. My mother is a teacher of theater arts, and my father works in airport security. My younger brother is nine years old, and he'll be going into fourth grade this fall. Sometimes he's a pest, but basically he's OK. We have a good time together. My older brother is in the army and is not home much. When he does return, he either eats or sleeps. There isn't much contact between us, but I love him very much.

Naturally, I fight with my parents. We haven't had a big one lately, but we always seem to be arguing. Usually my room is chaotic, and when my parents see what it looks like, they get irritated. They say, "Straighten up, straighten up," and I reply, "Tomorrow, tomorrow." Then nothing happens. Finally, the day comes when I'll need about three hours to clean everything up.

A few days ago my girlfriend was staying over at our home. Very late at night we started watching some movies. My father was angry that we were disturbing his sleep. He was upset that I was not being considerate, that there were dishes in the sink, and that I had brought a friend home to watch movies at five in the morning. But my parents don't interfere in my life too much. They're basically great about that. They don't prevent me from going to a show, even if it's in Tel Aviv. They make a face, but ultimately everything turns out OK. They know that I'll be coming back late—say, two in the morning. During vacation periods, I can go to sleep as late as five or six AM. Then I wake up at noon or one PM. That's not so bad. I have girlfriends who wake up at eight in the evening!

My family is not religious, and my parents don't observe Jewish traditions—almost not at all. But I do observe at least some of the rituals. On Yom Kippur our phone rings. I won't answer it, but they do. I also observe the tradition of fasting on that day. My family eats as usual. The smell of cutlets kills me. My mother prepares a butter puree with schnitzel, but I won't eat it, since I keep kosher.

My being religious began because of my brother, who became observant after his bar mitzvah. But I'm really not all that observant. I travel on the Sabbath, put lights on, and turn on the stove, but at Passover time I don't eat bread, though we have it in the house. My parents tell me that following tradition in this way is ridiculous. They view it as a temporary phase that I'm going through. For me, keeping traditions is important. We Jews are a nation that has kept itself going in exile for many years, and

"We Jews are a nation
that has kept itself
going in exile
for many years,
and what connects
us to one another
is our religion."

what connects us to one another is our religion. It's important to observe certain customs on holidays. I think it's a nice tradition to light candles and say the kiddush, the blessing over wine.

I love to sing. I'm in a choir, and I've been rehearsing a lot this summer. I love going abroad with the choir to participate in competitions, since I enjoy meeting people from different countries. One summer our choir flew to Spain, where we won first place in the competition. We were so good that we were invited to give a concert for peace the following year. This concert included music from the Jewish, Christian, and Muslim traditions—three religions, all together.

In school, I have a special liking for literature; I enjoy reading the poems of Natan Alterman. I write both poems and stories. I usually do my writing when I'm sad or bored. Although I don't really show my writings to others, there is an Internet site for creative writers, and I've put some of my writings on that site. People often respond to what they read there. I don't advertise the fact that my writings appear on the Internet, but if someone enters the site and responds, it's OK with me.

I study English and French in school. I decided not to study Arabic because it seems to me to be a language that's not especially useful. I have no connections to Arabs, and I'm not certain I want to have any connections in the future.

My life is very busy. I have so many things going that if I get to my homework before midnight, it's a miracle. For example, I was chosen to be the head of the student body in my school. I was so involved with so many activities connected to student government that I think I was absent from about half my classes.

I don't think that I was as good a president of the student body as I could have been. All in all I was quite disappointed with this experience. At the end of the year I went to our coordinator and told her that I thought the student body could do more than just arrange social activities. For example, we didn't address teacher-student relationships. At present, if a student has a problem with a teacher and wants to talk about it, the teacher often gets annoyed. The child then goes home, and nothing happens. Teachers and students don't make real eye contact in most cases. This problem is among the many issues that a student government should be dealing with.

Students should be allowed to take a stand on matters that are important to them. But no one really listens to us. The important thing about a student organization is that it has the possibility of developing leadership skills. And we all need to learn to take responsibility for what we're saying. This is important because kids in general don't take responsibility for the things they say.

I'm really not that interested in politics. Sometimes I read only the headlines, and I occasionally see the news on TV. I want peace, but it doesn't look to me like it will happen anytime soon. I am really upset about terrorism. It is preferable to have peace, but meanwhile, peace doesn't seem that close.

I love Israel very much. This love is something that's getting stronger in me. This was most obvious to me when we were in Germany. We had a parade with flags and sang in Hebrew, and I felt a lot of national pride. All of us felt that. We were the smallest choir, with only about twenty people. But when we displayed our flag, it was very emotional.

I have dreams about the future, but I don't think I'll be able to realize all of them. I just don't have much time. I know I will continue singing in a choir and playing the guitar.

CHAPTER 5

AHMAD

"I'm ready to share the land with people I don't like."

My name is Ahmad. I'm seventeen, and I live in Tira with my parents, two brothers, and one sister. I live in a neighborhood in Tira that doesn't have a special name. We can call it "Ahmad's neighborhood." It's located at the very end of the city, and it's just ordinary. Relationships with our neighbors are good, and we have lots of visitors in our home. I like the fact that everyone knows and likes one another. But we have a serious problem: The youth in the neighborhood have nowhere to go. We don't have any sort of clubhouse. We often wind up hanging out in a restaurant in the mall.

All my friends are male. I feel more comfortable with male friends. We can talk freely about sensitive matters. But I also like spending time with a group of girls. However, the society I live in does not encourage this practice. I feel envious when I see Israeli teenagers relating to their female friends.

In the summer our town is home to a continuous stream of weddings. Wedding parties become a place to go for teenagers. I myself don't like attending these weddings, because at wedding parties people often act in ways I feel are simply not appropriate. They celebrate all night. Everyone is invited, and everyone is burdened with the task of having to contribute money. When I marry, I'll arrange a simple wedding. I'll try to invite fewer people than is the norm. But I need to be realistic. In the end my father will do the inviting, and there's a custom that does not allow anyone to be excluded from the celebration.

I love my family. We spend lots of time together. When Israel allowed us to go to Jordan, the whole family traveled there. It was a great trip. But there are not only happy times in the family. When my grandmother died, our family understood what deep sadness feels like. My father happened to be in Tel Aviv when Grandma died. I phoned my father on his cell phone, but he didn't answer. When he did call back and I told him the news, he was devastated.

I don't like school. There are several dedicated teachers in my school, but the majority do not take their job seriously. These teachers just want to finish the day and go home. In my opinion the administration fails to

"Jerusalem should be a capital city for everyone:
Jews, Muslims, and Christians."

discipline our teachers. They seem out of control. They show a total lack of concern for us. I do have one favorite teacher. He teaches electronics and physics. Here's a teacher who's loyal to his students.

In the end our life here in Tira depends on the political situation. Peace between Palestinians and Israelis seems far off in the future. It will be difficult to achieve. Both parties are inflexible in many ways. For example, take the question of Jerusalem. The Jews want it only for themselves. This is certainly not a good thing. Jerusalem should be a capital city for everyone: Jews, Muslims, and Christians. Israel should have a different government. The policies of the Israeli government don't benefit either Israelis or Palestinians. The only ones who benefit are the settlers. Palestinians should unite and work closely with one another. I'm ready to share the land with people I don't like.

If someone were to give me a million dollars, I know exactly what I'd do with it. I'd donate a quarter of it to my secondary school. Then I'd build a place for the youth of Tira to gather. I'd also contribute to the mosque and to poor people. I would give the rest to my family.

CHAPTER 6

ALAA

"In the future I'd like to study medicine.
I expect there to be obstacles on my path to
becoming a doctor, but that won't divert me from my goal."

I'm Alaa Sultan. I'm sixteen years old and live in Tira. I will be entering eleventh grade in the local high school. Our family consists of my mom and dad, three daughters, and two sons.

I live in a big house in a neighborhood with a lot of new homes with fences around them. I feel free when I'm in the house or walking around in the neighborhood. I have lots of privacy. However, there's a negative side to all this. I feel isolated. There are no neighbors close to us and no girls my age nearby. Also, because of the limited municipality budget, we don't have any public parks to play in. That's why I spend most of my time in the house. There's not enough money because the government discriminates against Palestinians in this country. A lack of funds in the Palestinian community is the main cause of the suffering that's occurring in Palestinian cities within Israel.

There's a lot of warmth in my family. My parents are very supportive. Since I'm the oldest, when both my parents are busy, I'm not allowed to go out with my friends. I have to stay home and watch my brothers. And sometimes I'm not allowed to associate with certain ones of my girlfriends. My parents feel they dress in an unacceptable manner. We're Muslims, and for some of us dressing certain ways is just not tolerated. I understand and accept this form of interference in my life by my parents, but we in the family often argue among ourselves about exactly what kind of behavior outside the home is acceptable and what kind is not. Many parents, including mine, forbid girls from going swimming, playing basketball, going out to certain places, and coming home at certain times. When I'm a parent, I plan to allow my daughters to do some of these things.

I have some freedom when it comes to attending weddings. I even attend mixed weddings. I don't care if I dance on stage with boys and girls together, because everyone at the party is a relative. But I think we go to extremes with weddings. There's so much preparation. And so many people are invited. When I get married, I'll invite only a limited number of people.

I don't have a pet at home, although I like animals. Most Jewish

"I don't eat lamb, because when I was a little girl,
we took care of a lamb for a whole month.
During a holiday period we slaughtered it.
I loved that animal."

homes have a pet. Few of our homes have them. Dogs and cats demand that you spend a lot of time with them. They need constant attention. I guess we Palestinians don't have the time to do this. We don't want to take on that kind of responsibility.

When I was a little girl, my family took care of a lamb for a whole month. Then we slaughtered it as a sacrifice during the holiday of Eid Al Adha. I loved that lamb very much. Since that time I've not eaten lamb.

I have a best friend. She radiates optimism, and it's great to be with her. The only other friend I have who's like her is my mother. Both are good listeners, both listen to all my complaints, and both accept my opinions. I, too, accept everything they say to me.

About a year ago one of my friends, a classmate, died of cancer. We had an opportunity to participate in a project called "Knock on the Door." It was a project to raise money to fight cancer. My good friend and I tried to collect a lot of money. We went from house to house so that our class could contribute as much money as possible. We did this until late in the evening. I'm very proud of what we did—that I could be even of the smallest help in the fight against cancer.

Friendship isn't always smooth. Once I had a fight with one of my friends. We agreed to go out together to the mall to see a movie. It turned out that there wasn't enough room in the car for all of us, so I volunteered to stay home. My friend simply accepted what I had offered to do. It didn't seem to matter much to her that I wasn't getting to go to the mall! I was angry and felt that she was being very selfish. Finally, though, we talked about what had happened and got to understand one other.

I also have some male friends. In fact, most of the male students in my class are my friends. I don't get involved with them in social matters, however. We only discuss things related to schoolwork. I have mixed feelings about my school. Sometimes I'm just plain disappointed by what goes on. Once we were given a test for admission to a special program. I studied hard and got accepted. But it turned out that everyone who signed up for the test was accepted into the program— even those who didn't pass the exam. I was exasperated!

I like learning languages. Even though I'm in the science track, I read a lot of English. I enjoy reading a variety of authors. Shakespeare is a special favorite of mine. History is another matter altogether. Even though I sometimes like hearing about what's happened in the past—wars and things like that—when I think about having to sit for all the time needed to learn the material, I lose my enthusiasm.

My math teacher is my favorite teacher at school. I respect him a lot and appreciate him because he loves his students and knows how to teach in way that gets his ideas across to us. He also gives us the feeling that we're responsible for whatever happens in the classroom.

I also study Hebrew, but that's an obligation the state imposes on us. We're also forced to study the Bible. We study Torah and Jewish history more than Arabic and the Quran. This doesn't make sense.

I believe in God, even though I don't pray on a regular basis. But I do fast during the month of Ramadan. And I participate in discussions about matters related to the soul. Our religion teacher told us that the soul is always floating above us and sometimes comes to visit us. But I certainly don't like the fact that very religious people try to interfere with our daily lives. For example, my grandfather pesters me all the time not to do this and not to do that.

With regard to local politics, I know there's lots of corruption all around us. There's a common saying: "If you do this for me, I'll vote for you." They still haven't chosen the right people to lead our municipality. Our elections are based on clans, and we end up electing a relative.

As for the conflict between Israelis and Palestinians, I'm upset that the Israeli government controls the West Bank and the Gaza Strip. Palestinians are reduced to begging for the return of land that's theirs. Both peoples are paying the price of war. There are lots of casualties on both sides. So it's very important to solve this problem. If I were the head of the Israeli government, I'd withdraw to the 1967 lines in order to bring about peace and spare additional casualties.

In the future, I'd like to study medicine. Then I want to get married and have a daughter and other children. I expect there to be obstacles on my path to becoming a doctor, but that won't divert me from my goal.

CHAPTER 7

DANIEL

"If children
had been in
charge of
managing
their
countries,
things would
not have
happened the
way they did.
Children
know how to
get along
with one
another
despite
everything."

My name is Daniel Alon. I'm thirteen years old and live in Rishon LeZion with my mother, my stepfather, and my sister. I also have two stepbrothers who come to our home twice a week. I study at the preparatory school called "David Ben Gurion School." I'll be entering eighth grade this coming fall.

During my summer vacation, I attended a language course at the Technion University in Haifa. I also visited friends, swam in the swimming pool, and played on the computer. I spent a week and a half with my father. I went to work with him and came back home at seven or eight in the evening. And when I was in Rishon LeZion, there were several bar mitzvah celebrations. I had fun at those.

Many members of our family came to celebrate my bar mitzvah recently. During the ceremony, I was called upon to recite the blessings connected to reading the Torah. I felt that I had become an adult. I was among the first to recite the blessings. I felt proud to be part of my family at this ceremony. There were people from my father's family, from my mother's family, and from my stepfather's family. My father's family loves my mother. They don't ask why she left the marriage. They're just sad because of the divorce. I love both of my families very much.

I would like to be a parent myself sometime in the future. The most difficult thing in life is to be alone. I love children—sons especially. But I don't have problems with having daughters. The important thing is that I have healthy children who are also intelligent.

During the summer, I can't get to sleep till three o'clock or four o'clock in the morning. I want to sleep, but I just can't. By August I begin longing for the school year to begin. A one-month holiday is enough for me. I think that if the long vacation makes one miss school, it should be shortened. Perhaps some days could be added to our winter holiday. I miss playing soccer during recess at school. I'm looking forward to getting back to school so that I can be with my friends and see a few of my favorite teachers.

My favorite subjects at school are history, language, and literature. The subjects I dislike depend on the way teachers act toward their students. For example, I dislike math. I just didn't like the way the math teacher taught her subject. And I feel bored in English class, because my mother speaks English, and I've already learned the language. Arabic is a fun class because it's a new language for me. I don't speak Arabic, but if people talk with me, I can pretty much understand what they're saying. I received 100 percent in this class because the teacher is excellent. He motivates us to learn.

After school I listen to music when I need to calm down. I also play the piano. My mother has always wanted me to be a pianist. She actually forced me to study piano, and she hired a piano teacher to come to our home for lessons. You can bet the neighbors are pleased when I practice the piano at my father's home!

I've been at many weddings in my life, but what makes me nervous about attending a wedding is having to go and buy new clothes for the occasion. I don't like to shop. My mother knows what to buy. Usually I put on whatever comes out of the closet. I try to match the colors of the pieces of clothing I wear, but nothing ever seems to work.

I don't think about my own wedding celebration because I have time—another ten, thirteen, even twenty years. In the future I'd not like to move far away from my parents. I'd love to live in a place that is located halfway between where my parents live. For now, I'll stay in Rishon. I'm familiar with what it's like to live there everyday.

I know that I'm a Jew. My mother's grandfather suffered during the Holocaust. I don't ask my grandmother to tell about the Holocaust, but she often offers to talk about it with me. She managed to escape with her father. Hers was the only family in the area who survived. Stories about the Holocaust frighten me. Sephardic Jews from Arabic-speaking countries didn't suffer in the same way the Jews of Europe did. They didn't feel the pain, and because of this, some of them don't take the Holocaust as seriously as they should.

I have only a partial belief in God. Where is God? There was a war from 1939 until 1945. And where is God now? With the Palestinians? With the Israelis? With the Europeans? If there hadn't been a Holocaust, my belief in God would be stronger. I would be prepared not to travel on

**"Stories about the Holocaust frighten me.
Sephardic Jews from Arabic-speaking countries
didn't suffer in the same way the Jews of Europe did."**

the Sabbath. Religious people say that the Holocaust and all of Israel's wars occurred because people didn't believe in God. But to a great extent people *did* believe in God. If God doesn't help us in our time of need, he's not deserving of our dedication to him in our study of the Torah.

We have many ignorant religious people in our country, people who are just waiting for the coming of the Messiah. They pray instead of going to the army. Do you know how many children they have? In eleven years they'll have eleven children. Perhaps they can send their children to the army.

My father and I hold similar beliefs with regard to the political situation. I read lots of books, especially history books. I know that both Israelis and Palestinians have suffered. If children had been in charge of managing their countries, things would not have happened the way they did—and the way they still are happening. Children know how to get along with one another despite everything.

I came to know Palestinian children through a soccer club. I have one friend from a Druze family. Once I visited the home of a Muslim. I spoke Hebrew with the children of the family. We Israelis start to study Arabic only in the fourth grade, but Arabs start to study Hebrew in the first grade, so they know more Hebrew than we know Arabic. I played soccer with them. They told me they liked Maccabi Haifa.

I don't often argue with my mother about politics since I don't want to have an argument with her. For sure I'm for evacuating the settlements. They aren't part of Israel. I do think about the feelings of the settlers' children. Their parents chose to live there, and now it's become the children's problem, too. The settlers should be moved to southern Israel. Bedouin settlements could serve as models for them. I wouldn't be happy to have to force anyone to leave their homes, but we need to do something. Our region is not a fun place to be. If you want to go to the seashore, you're afraid that a suicide bomber will come up from under the water. So maybe forcing settlers to leave is not such a bad idea.

In my opinion, Jerusalem shouldn't be divided. The solution is to give the Palestinians only Gaza. If they don't accept this offer, they shouldn't even get Gaza. It would seem then that there's nothing to talk about with them.

CHAPTER 8

FIRAS

"My friends see
the computer as
merely a game.
For me, it's work!"

My name is Firas. I'm twelve years old, and I'm in the seventh grade. I have three sisters, two older and one younger. My father publishes a magazine called *Abeer*, and my mother works as a nurse. All around me are girls. Girls don't play boys' games. My little sister plays with her doll house, called "*Beit Beyoot.*" I ask her to come and play with me on the computer, but she refuses. I'd like to have a brother. A brother would play with me all the time.

I now live in Jerusalem, but my roots are in Arrabah, a town in the Galilee. Arrabah is more beautiful than Jerusalem. It's a small village, and I like small things. Jerusalem is a large city, and I can't get to know everything in it. In Arrabah I'm familiar with all the people and places. I feel it's my real home. On feast days and other big occasions, like weddings, I go back there. I like the wedding parties in Arrabah better than those in Jerusalem, because in Arrabah we get to dance the *dabka*. When I get married, I'll certainly arrange my wedding party to be like the ones in Arrabah. Many of my relatives who still live in Arrabah come to visit

**"We talk with them in Hebrew,
but they don't speak Arabic with us."**

us in Jerusalem. They ask me why I would ever want to come back to Arrabah. "Jerusalem is more beautiful," they say. I believe they're jealous of me because I'm living here. I answer, "You say this, but if you lived here, without friends, you'd want to return to Arrabah also." I add, as a challenge, "Let's change places. You come to Jerusalem, and I'll go to Arrabah."

Everyday I travel from Jerusalem to Wahat el Salaam, where I attend school. This school is different from others. There are both Palestinian and Israeli students in Wahat el Salam school. Israelis and Palestinians are friends at my school. Israeli students study Arabic in private lessons, but all they're studying is elementary Arabic, while we're doing more advanced studies in Hebrew. We speak Hebrew better than they speak Arabic. We talk with them in Hebrew, but they don't speak Arabic with us. We began our studies in religion just this past year. The Jewish students study about Judaism, and we study about Islam. Of all the teachers in the school, the Arabic teacher is my favorite. She listens to us and understands who we are. Most important, she doesn't scream.

In the afternoons, after school, I eat my dinner and then play on the computer. The computer is my best friend. I wouldn't care if all my friends go away as long as the computer stays close to me. When I was little—in first grade—my first computer had a game on it. I enjoyed playing that one game. Then, when no one was at home, I began experimenting with new programs. When I had questions, I'd ask my friends for help. But now I'm more skillful than they are. Now they ask me the questions. My friends see the computer as merely a game. For me, it's work!

In the evenings my father and I work together on the computer. I'd like to be a computer engineer when I grow up. I want to be like my father's friend who's knowledgeable about computers. He serves as a kind of model for me.

I'd prefer to have peace between the two sides of the conflict in our region. When there are problems between Palestinians and Israelis, the situation gets bad and has a terrible effect on the atmosphere in my school. There are Israeli boys who won't speak with us Palestinians for a while. But then we forget the problems, and we reconcile. When Al-Sheikh Ahmad Yasin was assassinated, we Palestinian students were angry and stopped speaking with the Israeli students. But after time passed, we became friendly again.

CHAPTER 9

ELINOR

"Once I ran into some Arabs,
and I spoke with one of them.
We really connected.
I realized that they're really like us."

I'm Elinor. I'm fifteen years old, and I live in Rishon LeZion, not far from Tel Aviv. My family consists of my mom and dad, my nineteen-year-old brother, and a dog.

My parents and I have a good relationship. When I need advice, they're there to give it to me. They listen to me when I have something to tell them. I always feel happy to be with my family. Just a few days ago, we all stayed at a hotel in Tel Aviv. My brother Tamir joined us a few days later.

Sometimes my mom gets angry if I arrive home late. I usually have to be home by eleven PM or midnight, but if I'm at the home of a friend who lives close by, I can come back later. My parents are very strict when it comes to how I take care of my room and where I can go with my friends. My parents' behavior doesn't always seem sensible to me. They just manage to get us accustomed to doing what they say. They tell us that we'll understand why these rules are important only when we ourselves become parents.

My brother is the kind of person you can talk to. We talk about friends and about what's worthwhile doing in life. He gives me good advice about school matters. Sometimes I do something, and he tells me that in the same situation he would have done something different. Tamir's personality is quite different from mine. He takes things less seriously than I do. Perhaps it's just different with boys. They don't make a big deal out of things. With girls, you are what you say. But I have to say that Tamir is a pretty understanding guy. Even though he's now in the army, we're still in close contact. In the beginning I couldn't talk to him when I wanted—only once a week or every two weeks. But now we're in more regular contact. If I need to, I call him at any hour of the day or night. Yet it's certainly strange to be at home without him, to be alone with my parents in the house.

I'm happy that my parents have taught me to care about others in need. A while ago I heard from a friend who let me know she was in distress. I sat in the park with her, and we talked at length. I was able to comfort her, reassuring her that the situation was not as bad as it seemed. I urged her not to abandon hope, and I advised her to return home to work on a solution to her problem. I felt especially proud that my parents had raised me to be what I am.

It's great to get up at ten o'clock during vacation periods. During the school year, I had to get out of bed at seven fifteen. But sometimes the summer vacation can be boring. It's not that I really want my studies to begin. I want school to start because I'm eager to see my friends. Yet after one week of school, I'll be asking, "When's vacation time?"

I have many girlfriends at this point in my life. When I finished ninth grade, everyone wrote something to me in our school yearbook. I've known each one of these friends for about ten years. My friends are like sisters to me. If they do something I think is wrong, I feel it's my duty to speak with them openly about it—and vice versa. This kind of honesty is an important part of what it means to be a friend to someone.

Sometimes it can be confusing to decide just who is your real friend and who is not. At other times it's pretty clear: There are friends you know you can rely on and those you know you can't. I have two friends whom I can really call *good* friends.

Once I was in an amusement park not long ago with a good friend. She dragged me on all the scary rides, and I was really grateful to her for doing that. If she had not urged me to be courageous, I would never

"Even though I'm unfamiliar with the lives of children in the Territories, it saddens me to hear about some eighteen-year-old who was killed there."

have gone on a mountain train. It's unbelievably scary, but I told myself that it was time I overcame my fear. My friend told me to start with a relaxation exercise. I did that, and then hugged and thanked her. After I had gone on the ride, I was so excited at what I had accomplished with my friend's help that I phoned my brother. What that girl did for me is the sign of a true friendship.

I generally like my studies at school. I'm not good in math, and I'm always working with my math teacher to avoid the possibility that I'll get a bad grade on my report card. In history, by contrast, I excel. And there were lots of humorous moments in my Bible class. The teacher was hilarious. She was young and made each of us feel that we were an important part of the class. That class was excellent. How I managed to do well in all my classes—including math—I'll never know. I can say that I've never gotten into trouble at school. Perhaps this has to do in part with the fact that my mother is a teacher and knows the other teachers and the principal well.

When I listen to the news, I always cry when I see the violence and when I hear about soldiers who were killed. I feel close to each and every soldier. It's scary when I hear about attacks that occur close to my city. Even though I'm unfamiliar with the lives of children in the Territories, it saddens me to hear about some eighteen-year-old who was killed there. I think all the killing is stupid. I feel like throwing up when I listen to an entire radio or TV news broadcast.

But I don't have any easy answers about resolving the conflict. Perhaps if everyone could know some of the things I know, the situation would improve. With regard to the disengagement, I think it's hard to move from place to place. If someone would tell me to evacuate my home, maybe I'd better understand what others are going through. All sorts of people's lives are being disrupted—even sacrificed—because of disputes that are basically clashes between leaders.

If I were in a mall and heard people speaking Arabic, I would not be afraid. What's the big deal? Are they going to kill me? Once I ran into some Arabs, and I spoke with one of them. We really connected. I realized that they're really like us. They do the same kinds of things we do—including some foolish things. They even dress like us. We're so similar. I have a friend who agrees with what I've just said and another friend who would disagree. I try talking to my friends about all that the two peoples have in common. But not all Palestinians are like those that I met. As is the case among every ethnic group, there are individuals of all kinds.

One time, as a school exercise, we had a mock Palestinian-Israeli trial. I was the lawyer for the Palestinian side. We had already studied some reasons why the Palestinians should have a land of their own. I found myself saying things that in my entire life I thought I would never say. I asked, "Why don't we Palestinians deserve our land?" It was scary being on the other side and facing the entire class during this exercise. I felt uneasy. I really didn't agree with all the things I had to say.

I also met an Arab girl at a seminar. Her father is a journalist, and her mother's a teacher. They all seem like nice people. If I were to go to her house, I'd be interested to see what her everyday life is like. But even without visiting her home, I can say that I believe she lives like me. If she were to come and visit me, I'd show her my home and many sites in the city where I live.

As for my future, I am going to be a therapist. I like to talk, and as a therapist, I'll get to meet lots of people. But first I'll spend two years in the army. Some young people plan to avoid going to the army. If you feel an obligation to the country—a deep sense of belonging—it becomes important to spend time in the army.

CHAPTER 10
HALA

"Because the Israelis are more powerful,
their suffering is always the big news.
It's the story that reaches the end of the world.
Every day ten of us are killed,
and no one talks about it, even in the daily news."

My name is Hala. I'm sixteen years old, and I live in Sheikh Jarah in East Jerusalem with my mother, father, and grandmother. I have one sister and one brother, both older than I am. They're both studying abroad now.

My parents don't share the same religion. Mom is a Christian and Dad's a Muslim. That doesn't make a difference in our family. It's nice to have parents from two religious traditions. It's also very beautiful to have celebrations from both religions. We celebrate Eid Al Adha, Christmas, and Easter. We decorate the Christmas tree, and all of us—including my mother—fast on Ramadan.

From both home and school, I've learned there is no difference between people and no core differences among the various religions—Buddhism, Judaism, Christianity, Islam, and so on. A human being is a human being. There is no need to know that this one is a Muslim and that one a Christian—as if this one were black and this one white.

Unfortunately, the world is full of discrimination and stereotyping. Till this day such discrimination persists. When I go to Europe and say I'm an Arab, immediately people say I must be a Muslim. They don't even know that there are Christian Arabs. In Europe they think that we have camels and ride to school on them. I tell them, "No, we have cars." Last January I was in London. Some people asked, "Where are you from?" I told them, "I'm from Palestine." They asked, "From Pakistan?" They just don't recognize Palestine until I mention the word "Israel." Then they think I'm an Israeli. I say, "No, I am a Palestinian."

When I go to a Jewish area, they also don't believe I'm an Arab, and when I talk in English they're astonished that I don't speak Hebrew, and that I don't study Hebrew at school. I never used to say that I was a Palestinian in front of Israelis, but my sister is proud of being a Palestinian. She tells everyone that she's Palestinian. She always tells me "You have to be proud to be a Palestinian." When my sister mentions that we're Palestinians in the presence of Israelis, I feel that they begin to look at us differently. Their looks become not nice, or they just turn away and leave us. I tell them that Palestinians are not people to be afraid of. Are we a threat to that extent?

I'm studying ballet at a new cultural center in a Palestinian area of East Jerusalem. I'm glad that there is such a center. I go there four times a week and at the end of the week I go shopping there with my friends. We shop only in the Palestinian area. For the last year and a half we haven't gone to a mall in a Jewish area.

I attend the Anglican School in West Jerusalem. I'll be entering the eleventh grade this fall. At the Anglican school we have a choice to study Arabic, Hebrew, Spanish, or French. I study Arabic. Dad always says, "Read, read." If I want to live here in this country after finishing my university studies and if I want to work as an attorney, I'll need to know literary Arabic. But it's a strong possibility that I'll continue my studies in England. I have uncles there, and I'm familiar with the country.

I will not study in an Israeli university. I know someone who went to study at a college in Herzelia, a town in Israel. He wrote a long letter to the president of the university because on one occasion the university had displayed the flags of all countries except for the flag of our country, Palestine. The president didn't reply and began acting with some hostility toward this student. This student used to go to parties with all the students at the college. But after they discovered that he was a Palestinian, they gradually began to turn their back on him.

Including me, there are only three Palestinian students in my school. The rest of the student body is made up of international students. They come from lots of places, like the Philippines, Italy, America, Romania, Sri Lanka, and Finland. I see how they think, I hear how they talk, I see how they dress and the kinds of food they eat. That's to say, I'm aware of the differences in cultures. These students are different from me. There's a difference in their parents' thinking. Many students stay out late in the night, drink, smoke, and do things that we Arabs don't do. For example, they don't have many restrictions about the time they have to return home. It's difficult for them to understand my culture.

But my relationship with some of these students is very good. I talk with them as if I were speaking with Arabs. However, when they talk about politics, everything gets distorted. The students who live in the Jewish area say, "See how fearful of Arabs the Jews are!" In this case I just can't reply because if I did, it would start an argument. Three years ago, I received an e-mail about the Intifada with photos of murdered Palestinians. I innocently sent it to my classmates. A boy sent me this reply: "Go to Hell, Hala"—as if I had done something shameful. I didn't mean to upset anyone. I was only showing them photos of how the Jews were torturing us.

I have one very close friend. She's like me. We have the same friends, and my family loves her. Once she was very upset. Her father had died seven years ago, and it was the anniversary of his death. I didn't know that, and I left her in a way that she felt was abrupt. She got angry at first but then she came to see me and told me what was happening. I started to cry with her because people whom I've loved have also died. I admire how she handled this. I'm not as good at telling what's bothering me. When I have a problem with somebody, I just can't talk to them. I keep it all inside, and it continues to hurt. Sadly for me, my friend has just left for Colorado, and since she left, I feel alone. I'm very sensitive. I don't really want to change who I am, but I would rather not be so sensitive.

Even though friendship is so important, I have to say that my main support comes from my family, especially my parents. My mom and I are very close. Both parents are always there for me. Two years ago my cousin died in London. I was there and saw firsthand how he suffered. Two months later, my friend—who was also my neighbor and school-mate—died as well. My father's aunt who lived with us had also died the same year, so I wound up being emotionally exhausted. Through all this my parents continually comforted me. My sister and brother also support me. I talk about life issues with them. My brother and I kid around together all the time. Sometimes I feel he understands me better than my sister. But I love them equally.

I go to a peace camp called "Peres for Peace." The director is an Israeli. Both Israelis and Palestinians attend the camp. Both sides say they're suffering. The Jews admit that we, the Palestinians, suffer more than they're suffering. Last year all the Israeli participants in the camp reached the age of eighteen and had to go to the army. So we needed a new group of Israelis to join us. Once we had a meeting in which Jewish girls and boys started crying and saying, "No, we don't do these horrible things to the Palestinians." The director tried to calm them down, but they were saying that they didn't believe that Jews had done the things we Palestinians were describing. They said, "We hate you, we've never done anything bad to you except if you did something bad to us or tried to kill us." They just don't know anything. No accurate information gets to them. We watch Israeli, American, and European TV, and the first item on the news is how a Palestinian has blown himself up. They fail to report that "Today, a Palestinian was killed, a Palestinian house was demolished, and a farm was destroyed."

Because the Israelis are more powerful, their suffering is always the big news. It's the story that reaches the ends of the world. Every day ten of us are killed, and no one talks about it, even in the daily news. Because of this I don't try to discuss the conflict with the Israeli partic-ipants at the camp. I know that if I give them my answers, there will be a riot. I prefer to be silent, because they're not ready to listen and to understand. They won't change their minds.

Since I was seven years old I've wanted to be a lawyer. Many people have discouraged me about my plan, but I won't change my mind. I'd like to go to court and defend people. I'm strong and can stand my ground against my opponents. Also there's a lawyer I saw in a film called *Legally Blonde*. She was a young woman, always with her dog in the courtroom and always wearing rosy-colored clothes. I liked her dress, the way she wore a jacket and blouse under it, the way she carried her bag, and the way the heels of her shoes tapped the floor. It was a nice feeling. I imagine myself like her, entering the court with strength. I don't possess that kind of strength as yet.

CHAPTER 11
ELLA

"And when I grow up, I want to have lots of children— maybe three or four."

I'm Ella Shik, and I live in Tel Aviv. I'm twelve years old. I live with my mother and a brother who's almost seventeen. I'll be entering sixth grade in Bialick School this fall.

My girlfriend and I like to skate on the roof of a neighborhood home together—using water and soap to provide a slippery surface. We also like to play tricks on people who are passing by in the street. We spray them with water guns.

I live in a Tel Aviv neighborhood called "Florentine." It's a strange place to live, full of uneducated children. If I were to become mayor of Tel Aviv, I'd make certain that there were houses that had yards with grass in them. But in Tel Aviv you can find good places to go to even now. I love the beach, the park, and the city center.

But when I grow up, I've decided I will not live in Tel Aviv. I'd like to live on a kibbutz. What attracts me most about kibbutz life is that I'd get to spend time in nature. I love everything that's green. While I spent some time as a guest on a kibbutz, I studied at a school for dogs who were being trained to help blind people and pensioners. These dogs were learning things like how to bring newspapers to elderly people. In the future I'd like to train dogs to do things like that.

Recently, while I was on a trip to the Sinai Peninsula, I was put in charge of a pregnant dog. Finally, she gave birth to two puppies. Someone found one of the puppies buried in the sand. I pulled him out, put a blanket on him, and gave him milk. He survived, and I felt good about myself.

My grandmother lives in Hungary. It bothers me that she forgot to call and congratulate me on my birthday. I'm angry with her. I won't speak to her at all—not only because of what happened on my birthday, but also because she often does a number on me. My grandmother makes fun of me. Every time I visit her with my brother, she says, "What a handsome boy you are"—as if I didn't exist. I feel that I don't care any longer whether or not I have a grandmother.

I used to have a strong fear of earthquakes—really something that could be called a phobia. It began when I was younger. There was an

"I'd like to make our world a safe place to live in."

earthquake while I was in school one day. The teachers and administrators told us to move quickly to a special room. I didn't understand what was happening. When I was informed that it was an earthquake, I felt so scared that I became ill and had to go home. That's how it all began. But I sought help, and now I've overcome the phobia.

I'd like to make our world a safe place to live in. Right now, we Israelis feel insecure because of all the attacks. We needed to evacuate our school recently because of a suspicious object that was discovered inside the building. This was the second time we had to leave school. Everyone is stressed when this happens. And it always seems to happen at the end of the year when there's a party going on.

If I were in charge of the country, I would try to make peace. There are good Palestinians and bad Palestinians. Some Palestinians think we're evil, too. We blow up something and they blow up something. I would put an end to this kind of warfare. I don't want to deal with gas masks all the time or to have there be drills in school or to have to go to shelters.

I have many dreams for the future. I would want my mother and father to be together again. I'd want to join a chorus. And when I grow up, I want to have lots of children—maybe three or four. I also think about what I'd like to happen right away. Right now I want there to be fewer social problems in the country and fewer family problems at home. And I want to successfully complete my elementary school education. I'd like to be independent in all aspects of my life.

CHAPTER 12

HANEEN

"When it comes to doing work at home, my parents know
that I'm the oldest and that I should do more of the work.
But when they give presents, they forget that
I'm the one with all the responsibilities."

My name is Haneen. I'm sixteen years old, and I live in Yama in Al-Muthalath. Our family consists of four girls and one boy. My mother is an English teacher. I feel happy when we're all together as one family, especially when my father is home, because he works outside the home all the time. It's a special time when we're sitting around the breakfast table and my father is with us. Most of our neighbors are our relatives. They're my grandparents, uncles, and cousins. I have good relationships with all of them.

I'm the oldest girl in the family. My mother always tells me how hard it is to be in that role. I have to serve as a model for my sisters and brother. And every mistake is remembered, as it were, as part of an "account." I like my family, but I wish I had an older brother. I'm carrying a heavy load—a lot of responsibility—and I don't want it. I'm also annoyed when my mother scolds me in front of my little sisters. Also during feast days, they give me the same amount of money that they give my sisters. I should be given more because I'm the oldest. When it comes to doing work at home, my parents know that I'm the oldest and that I should do more of the work. But when they give presents, they forget that I'm the one with all the responsibilities. When they give, they give the same, but when they take, they take more.

There's always some fighting going on among us siblings. I quarrel with Tasneem, who's one year younger than I am. We always quarrel about small things. For example, I don't like to give her my clothes to wear. I don't like to lend her my things because she's not responsible. She doesn't care if they become dirty. She'll sit wherever she wants while she's wearing them. That makes me mad. I warn her about keeping my clothes clean, but she doesn't seem to care. This irritates me further.

I attend Yama secondary agricultural school. It's a large school. At first I wasn't happy when I had to transfer from ninth grade to this comprehensive school. When you transfer to a new school, they subject you to a lot of examinations. That can be boring.

I don't have a close girl friend in my new school at the present time. Most of my girl friends are from my town or the town nearby. I have one especially good friend who lives in Jatt. I like her character, her sincerity. We never get angry at each other. The twenty-third of August was my birthday. She and my other friends made me a birthday party. It was a complete surprise. I was delighted when I walked in and saw everyone there.

I don't have good friends of the other sex. But I am friendly with the boys in my class. I'm not interested in them becoming a part of my group of close friends, but I feel comfortable with them. They're not that different from us. I'm especially impressed by one boy who can recite seventeen parts of the Quran by heart. I spend time talking with him about our schoolwork and our psychometric exams.

There should be mutual trust among friends. Friendship means you're feeling comfortable with someone. I would never betray a friend who told me a secret unless there was something crucial that I felt had to be revealed. In that case I'd ask my mother's advice as to whether or not to tell.

Most of the things my friends and I talk about concern the subjects we're studying in school. We also talk about some of the girls and about the teachers. Sometimes, I dislike a teacher at the beginning of a school year. But after a few more classes, I'll come to like him. In general I like all my teachers. But there's one language teacher in my school who I believe is unfair to students. He gives special attention to a certain girl who is really fluent in the language she's studying. We talk about this teacher, how he neglects all our other classmates and gives most of his attention to this one girl. For example, we all have an opportunity to attend summer school abroad. A teacher is required to inform everyone in his class about that opportunity, but this teacher gave the information to this one girl alone. She was accepted in the school and has left for England. I told my mother and father about what had happened. My father warned me not to get involved, not to go and inform the principal.

I love math. It's my favorite subject. When I'm doing math problems, I feel happy. It makes my brain work. I also like learning languages because it helps me in my daily life and familiarizes me with the lives of people of other nations. I study Arabic, English, and Hebrew. Eng-

"Islam asks us to behave with integrity and to love people without considering their color, race, or religion."

lish is the most important language in the world because it's the language of America, the world's strongest country.

I love being a Muslim. My model in life is the Prophet Muhammad. He's our leader, our ideal person. I pray the five prayers daily and fast on Ramadan. However, I don't recite the Quran very much. When I'm tense about something, I begin praying so that I can feel some relief from the stress I'm feeling. Islam is built on certain principles that serve as the basis for guiding our behavior toward others. Islam asks us to behave with integrity and to love people without considering their color, race, or religion. It's enough that he's a human being!

There are some wonderful customs in our tradition, such as what occurs at weddings. When a bride and groom are happy, it seems as if all the world shares their joy. When I get married, my wedding will follow the traditional customs. I'll invite all my friends and family. The groom I choose should be educated, should pray, fast, and be a pious man.

However, there are a few customs I don't especially like. Having no equality between girls and boys is unfair. I also dislike not being able to study abroad and not being able to come home late at night. My parents may allow me to study abroad, but tradition will affect their decision.

With regard to the conflict with Israelis, if someone on the other side does something wrong, I don't regard the whole nation as responsible for that one person's acts. I don't like the prime minister. He's an unjust person. He doesn't care about others, especially children. If I were in his place, I'd make peace between Palestinians and Israelis. I'd help both peoples come close to one another. But it would be a heavy burden to be in his place.

I want to be a doctor. It's a good job. I can really help people if I practice medicine. I would like to work in pediatrics. If I can't study here, I'll go abroad. Perhaps I'll study in a nearby country, like Egypt or Jordan. If I become wealthy, I'll donate money to our people in the West Bank. And I'll give money to the Al-Aqasa Association that adopts orphans and cares for them.

Even though there are different nationalities, customs, and religions in the world, my hope is that there will be a lasting peace.

CHAPTER 13

MAOR

"Giving just seems like the right thing to do— always."

I'm Maor Zetun. I'm fifteen years old, and I live in Rishon LeZion with my mother, my father, an eleven-year-old brother, Aviv, and another brother, Natan. I'm the oldest. Being a big brother is a heavy responsibility. I feel I'm not just occupying space in the family. I'm concerned about the welfare of my brothers. I worry about them. But it's not always smooth with Aviv. I don't feel comfortable when he stares at me while I'm having a meal. Let him look at me at other times, not when I'm eating. It's unpleasant and it's embarrassing. He also tells his friends things I've confided to him. This is one reason I appreciate my father. I tell him my secrets, and he doesn't reveal them to anyone, even my mother. I'd like to be like him when I grow up.

Recently the whole family traveled to Amsterdam. In Holland I felt my parents were watching over me, protecting me. I sensed—in a special way—that we're a family. It was a great feeling.

I'm in ninth grade in school. I love my studies in biology and Arabic. Biology is needed in today's world. Today everything is based on technology. Every day there are new scientific developments in the world. As for my Arabic studies, I can say that it's a fascinating language. What makes it special for me is that my grandma came from Turkey, a Muslim country. Also, my Arabic teacher is an excellent instructor. An excellent teacher, in my opinion, is one who understands you and has faith in you, even when you're not so successful in your studies. As a result every lesson becomes interesting.

During summer vacations I miss school. Not my studies, but my school friends. I have tons of friends. The majority are males. Girls in my class tend to fight and curse each other. You have to be generous toward your good friends. Giving just seems like the right thing to do—always.

When I think about the future, I know I'd like to be rich. I'll do whatever will give me the most money at the end of the day. If I were to become wealthy, I'd use the money to help build hospitals and to help people who don't have a house. I'd also like to help the Palestinians, as long as they don't use my money for negative purposes.

I have a dream that there will someday be peace and that we'll get along with the Palestinians. The settlers feel that where they're living is *their* place, but in order to have peace, you have to give up something. I believe we have to give up the Territories, even though it hurts a lot to do that. If a child from a settlement were to disagree with me, I'd say that we just can't continue to live the way we've been living.

Every day someone gets hurt. Israel has to care about the safety of

"I'd like to meet other Palestinian children. I'd like to learn about their family life and, in general, get to know them well."

its citizens. When I travel anywhere by bus, I look at everyone who gets on. I sit facing the door. I want to stop being fearful. I want to stop looking at the front door of the bus.

A lot of people around me say we have to kill Palestinians. That's sad. Palestinians are human beings. I don't think it's right to talk about killing Palestinians. Here's the problem: If you go to a place and settle there, and then someone comes and takes the place from you, you can't say who's right. But you need to solve the problem, you have to start negotiating.

I once met a Palestinian boy living within Israel. He didn't know what to say to me because it seemed to me that he had been brainwashed. But I'd like to meet other Palestinian children. I'd like to learn about their family life and, in general, get to know them well. I'm really not sure what Palestinian children eat. Perhaps it's lamb. I know they enjoy eating meat.

CHAPTER 14

IBRAHEEM

"When I pray,
I set myself
away from the
world for a
few moments."

M y name is Ibraheem. I live in Jatt Al-Muthalath with my mother and father, and three sisters, Amnah, Iman, and Salma. Iman is twelve years old, and Salma is ten and a half. My family always stands behind me. They only have positive things to say about me. When I sat for the psychometric examination, I received a grade that was good, but not excellent. I received the full support of my family at that time.

My neighbors are also supportive. I like the fact that there are neighbors living close to me. In my neighborhood, people are concerned for one another. If someone here becomes sick or needs something, people are right there to take care of him. But my village is very crowded. When I get older, it's possible that I'll continue to live in my home village, but there's a strong probability that I'll go abroad.

At school, I have to say that I really like tests. Most students are more interested in getting a good grade than they are in learning the material. Physics is my favorite subject at school. I can grasp it quickly. The last theory we studied was Newton's idea that every action has a reaction. However, the facilities for studying physics at our school are very limited. Our last experiment dealt with free-falling objects. But there are also some subjects I don't like to study, like urban science. Urban science deals with lots of facts, like state laws. This kind of learning just doesn't appeal to me.

I have good friends at school, but we don't form a clique of any sort. Friendship, to me, means cooperation. The most important thing about friendship is that when someone needs help, his friend is there to help him. If a close friend were seriously ill and needed a kidney transplant, I would give him one of my kidneys. But I wouldn't give him both, because I don't want to die. And, of course, if a friend needed money, I'd be ready to lend it to him. I would never charge interest. I don't believe in it. I also have female friends at school. The one closest to me is an active, helpful person. After school and during vacation periods, I visit my friends. Actually, the closest of my friends lives only ten meters away. We listen to songs on the computer together, and we chat over the Internet.

I'd like to be famous in the future, either in a scientific field or in engineering. I'd like to study at the Technion in Haifa. If I'm accepted, I'll begin right away. If I'm not accepted, I'll submit my application a second time and then wait a year.

I practice karate. I have a brown belt, and I'm working hard to get the black belt. We organize karate matches in the region. I took the second rank. But karate is just my hobby. I wouldn't, for example, try out for the Olympics. If I were selected to represent Israel, I wouldn't participate, even if I had the chance to do so. What I love about karate is the discipline. This is the same discipline I get from practicing my faith.

I like fasting in the month of Ramadan, the month of forgiveness. I pray all the time. When I pray, I set myself apart from the world for a few moments. For a while, my head is relieved of worries about what's going on in the world. I also believe strongly in paradise and hell. This belief affects my daily actions. But Islam is not mainly about fear. Fear of hell helps me resist doing evil deeds. But it's the love of paradise that motivates me to engage in good actions. Although the Quran emphasizes the need to obey one's parents, I'm by no means a perfect Muslim in this regard. Sometimes I don't listen to what my father tells me to do. I feel sometimes that he wants to micromanage me. I love him, but I resent that about him.

I love the Arabic language, and I like reading stories in Arabic. I read a book that includes a story about the struggle of a Palestinian girl with the chains put around her by the society she's living in. It's about certain restrictions in her life. She can't do whatever she wants or be with whomever she wants, because society may come to regard her as different. I sympathize with her struggles. When I get married and have children, I'll want to give them a little more freedom than I have in my family. For instance, I'm not allowed to listen to songs on the radio or on TV. I would want to let my children listen to songs and watch television.

This girl's story reminds me a lot of my own life in my neighborhood and in other villages close by. I wrote a report on this book for school. I was able to publish it on the Internet. Publishing on the Internet has both a positive and a negative side. The person can publish whatever he wants to, right or wrong. But to be able to express different points of view is a very good thing.

If I were in charge of the Israeli government, I'd give Jerusalem to the Palestinians. The Palestinians have the right to establish a country for themselves, a country liberated from Occupation. The Israelis would have a country with fixed borders also. I'd make the two sides equal, which isn't the case now.

There's no constitution in Israel, although there are basic laws. Because there's no constitution, the government can discriminate against minorities and govern them any way they want. Were there a constitution, I don't think they would be able to do that.

CHAPTER 15

MATAN

"I think that a
desire to study
certain subjects
springs from
natural curiosity.
I'm just not
interested in
having someone
limit my range
of possibilities."

My name is Matan. I'm sixteen years old, and I live with my mother and two brothers. I study at an open democratic school in Jaffa. An open democratic school is a school in which you can choose what you're going to study and the methods you'll be using to learn the subjects you've chosen. You're personally involved in everything that happens at the school. At the beginning I was overwhelmed by all the changes from what I was accustomed to. I had to adapt to this new kind of school structure.

In making the decision to go the open school, I had to think hard about why I was dissatisfied with my previous traditional school. "Why," I asked myself, "did this kind of alternative school suit me?" I concluded that it was very difficult for me to understand why I was being taught the way I was in my former school. I realized that I wanted to think in a more global way. I think that a desire to study certain subjects springs from natural curiosity. For example, it's very easy for me to solve math problems. But no one at my new school will tell me, "Stop doing math because you're good at it." I'm just not interested in having someone limit my range of possibilities. I've had conflicts with those who have tried to impose limits on me in the past.

In my first year at the open school I had a conflict. At the age of fourteen I came in contact with political groups, and I was exposed to some new ideas. Usually people just don't wake up at all, but at this point I can say that I'm trying hard to be awake politically. My brother was stationed as a soldier in Lebanon, and I think that reflecting on his experiences was the beginning of my awakening. My brother came back home from Lebanon, and after listening to his experiences, I did a lot of serious thinking. And I think my new political awareness has changed me. I've become more mature than other members of my age group.

When you're young—say, seven years old—no one brings up these kinds of political issues. I remember thinking, at the age of six, about what I'll be when I grew up. At that time all I thought about was being in the army. I remember in fifth grade that when I watched the news on TV, I shouted, "Why are the stinking Arabs doing things like this? What have we done to them?" Terrible things followed. Young Palestinians fought against our soldiers. I used to ask everyone, "What's happening? A Palestinian child is living here. For that child, living in this place is his way of realizing the essence of his being." But at age twelve, I was really not so concerned about all this. It was just something painful to be seen on the television news. A terrible war was going on. But until I learned about my brother's experiences in Lebanon and about the work of Peace Now, I was really not aware of what was happening.

I think we have to look at the whole picture. What's going on inside me does not have to do with whether or not I like Arabs. I see that people are living under Occupation, so I feel I have to help them. We live in a world in which human beings seem to have lost the possibility of establishing personal connections with one another. But I believe that we don't have to live this way. I can make my own judgments about the situation.

Once several of us participated in a demonstration. We talked for

**"A person should be loyal to his principles,
but there's something more important which he has to do:
He must be ready to criticize his own views."**

three hours with some soldiers. Some Palestinians came to hear what we were talking about. I said to an Israeli soldier: "Look at this Palestinian, do you consider him a terrorist? Ask him. Perhaps he'll tell you he's not."

Two weeks ago I traveled to Italy for a seminar, and we talked about how Palestinians believe that they should have the right to return to their land. The Israelis said that we have our own ideas about this matter. But for there to be any hope for a solution, they were prepared to accept the possibility that at least some Palestinians could return to Israel.

I understand a settler when he says that the Torah is holy. I also understand a person when he tells me that the Quran is holy. There is still the possibility of a relationship here. Everyone has his own point of view. If a Palestinian wants to live with us, agrees not to hurt us, and accepts the fact that he'll be living under the laws of Israel, let him come. I don't have a problem with this. The issue is that the settlers want to realize their own ambitions at the expense of others. They have a unique set of beliefs. A person should be loyal to his principles, but there's something more important which he has to do: He must be ready to criticize his own views. There's more danger in not criticizing yourself than there is in not being loyal to your principles.

I've visited a Palestinian village that I liked. This visit symbolized the possibility of a successful relationship between Israelis and Palestinians. But the wall being built by Israelis—supposedly to protect Israelis within the pre-1967 borders—has eliminated approximately one thousand dunams of Palestinian land. There are people who have the courage to stand in front of the bulldozers all the time. Soldiers shoot at them. I participated in one of these demonstrations. I personally witnessed who attacked whom. I was there. The soldiers used tear gas. This experience gave me an excellent opportunity to examine the conflict from both sides.

I talked with the demonstrators about how they viewed the conflict, about how they thought it could be resolved. We also discussed personal matters. One can always find personal things to talk about. Talking in this way leads to a truly *human* relationship—in the fullest sense of that word. Even now, these demonstrators and I have connections that are personal.

I'm a member of an organization called "Anarchists Against the Wall." Anarchism means that every individual should be acknowledged for who he is. Every individual has his own needs. Anarchism asks, "What does the state and the individual have in common? What interests do they share?" I'm an individualist. I accept philosophies that come from the perspective of an individual—the fruit of his own world vision. There's no problem with pluralist thinking. I've been influenced by the writings of Marx and Mao, and I spend lots of time writing down my ideas about politics so that others will know about them and learn who I am. I really want to study philosophy when I'm older, perhaps in England or France.

What I've said doesn't mean I'm not connected to my Jewish roots. I feel myself to be Jewish. I feel this especially when I read about the Holocaust. I feel a connection between what was done to us then and what's happening in the country now. What I'm attached to is the culture of Judaism and its values. Even though I don't agree with everything written in the Torah, the values found there are important. There are lots of things in the Torah that are not adhered to by the State of Israel.

A final word about the conflict: I don't believe in state control, I don't believe in the authority of the nation-state. If we continue building a wall, we'll be freeing ourselves from our moral responsibilities. We'll be destroying the economy of the Palestinians. Any attempt at coexistence will come to an end.

I find it hard to envision where I'll be and what I'll be doing in the next ten or twenty years. I see that our society has to work on itself and eliminate hatred from our midst.

CHAPTER 16

JAD

"Friendship means feeling truly satisfied when you're with that person whom you consider your friend."

I'm Jad. I'm sixteen years old, and I live in Bakah El-Garbiah. I have a brother, Safi, who is fifteen years old, and a sister, Ward, who is three.

I enjoy spending time with my family. All of us love outdoor activities and trips away from home. Once we went to Tiberius for three days. It was a wonderful experience. I also had a good time when we all went on a trip to Sharm al-Sheikh. But the most intriguing experience of all was when my brother and I traveled to Kenya with our father. There we went on safari and were able to get very close to wild animals.

I can't remember an unhappy moment in my family. Every day has its joyous moments. Even family rules—not to play on the computer more than two hours a day or not to stay up late when there's school the next day—don't reduce my happiness. I accept and approve of these rules. Even though they cause discomfort and annoy me, I realize they're important.

I study in the Orthodox College in Haifa. My school is the most important thing in my life. My favorite subjects are chemistry and biology, but I also like English. The school has an excellent reputation. Students here have a promising future. It's also good to have the opportunity that this school provides to meet new people from a variety of places.

In my old school in Bakah I never saw a boy and a girl sitting together around the same table in the classroom. Bakah is a conservative town. In my new school, we have lots of freedom. Teachers treat us with more respect, and students have rights. But I still have good relationships with my former classmates in Bakah, and we spend a lot of our time together.

I have a small group of friends at school. We laugh, tease each other, and joke around a lot. My closest friends are boys. I'm friendly with girls but not in the sense of having a "girlfriend." To me, friendship means feeling truly satisfied when you're with that person whom you consider your friend. And friends should always tell the truth to one another and shouldn't get angry at each other when they have different views on issues. My best friend is still studying in Bakah. I tried to convince him to transfer with me to Haifa, but his family was frightened. There have

**"Palestinians need wise leaders who have the ability
and the competence to negotiate with Israel."**

been explosions in Haifa, and his family was afraid that the political situation was too unstable for them to allow their son to go that far away and stay in a big city.

My family has allocated a budget for my time at school, but when I need extra money to go out with my friends, I ask my father for more. I'm always open with him. I tell him where I'm going, and if I change my plans, I just call him on my cell phone. It's really necessary to have a cell phone. It's especially important because I'm in Haifa so much of the time. The cell phone allows me to stay in touch with my family.

After school, I swim, play volleyball, or listen to music. I also enjoy playing the piano. I play the music I most often listen to, but I don't have any dreams about becoming a famous musician. I dream of becoming a famous basketball player someday. I've been playing point guard, both distributing the ball to other players and shooting it myself.

I know that you have to practice continually in order to be a famous basketball player. However, I don't have access to decent facilities and coaches. The Bakah municipality doesn't care about building sports facilities where teenagers can practice. Sports are simply neglected. The kibbutzim and Jewish towns surrounding Bakah all have very beautiful, modern sport facilities, but I can't go there to practice. Most local leaders in Bakah have corrupt agendas and focus on private interests. The head of our municipality should pay attention to how the youth of our town are educated. He should care about our future. His administration should build clubs and playgrounds for the young people of the community. When I think about the future, I see myself traveling abroad, if I can, since living and prospering in Bakah is hard.

I wish the political situation between Israelis and Palestinians would improve. Then our social and economic life would improve in Bakah. True, Palestinians and Israelis do get a chance to meet in the cities, like Tel Aviv, Hadera, or Haifa. However, they see one another in commercial buildings or at recreational sites. No real social relationships form between them. Instead, a wall separates both communities.

Palestinians need wise leaders who have the ability and the competence to negotiate with Israel. The Palestinian people are weary and disheartened. They don't ask for their rights. They just accept the tyranny of their leaders.

If I don't succeed in becoming a professional basketball player, I have other dreams. I would like to be an astronaut or to work in the field of chemistry, where I would invent something great and become the wealthiest man in the world.

CHAPTER 17
NADIA

"The Palestinians
demand a
homeland.
They want
a place to live.
We were also
that way once.
We did not have
a state, a place
to return to."

My name is Nadia Shir. I'm fifteen years old, and I live in Jerusalem with my mother and father. My father was married and had two daughters before I was born. My half sisters are twenty-eight and thirty-one. I have good relationships with them. I really don't think of them as half sisters. They're like regular sisters. But people tell me they're just half sisters.

I think a lot about divorce. Rather than fighting all the time in front of their children, parents would do better to live in separate homes. Couples keep trying to get along, thinking they can keep their problems secret from the rest of the family. The situation becomes like a circle you can't escape from. Sometimes people just do not get along, and they should be able to resolve their problems by going their separate ways.

I attend an experimental high school. We have many innovative programs. The teachers try as much as possible to take students' interests into account. My school promotes the values of the Labor Movement. I'm not sure that it really has those values; it may just be a "put on." Yet I feel that this is a different kind of school. The teachers try to instill in us the value of treating people equally. There's a lot of personal contact in school, and the teachers really care about us. Every one of us is personally involved in what's going on.

I'll be entering tenth grade in the fall. I've chosen a track in which we concentrate on sociology, psychology, and anthropology. I like analyzing human beings. I like learning about what they think and how their thoughts are connected to the culture they're living in. My mother says I have a deep understanding of other people. She once read a book about Freud, and said to me, "Wow, this is hard." I asked her, "What's hard?" She explained to me that Freud had analyzed a woman's dream. She then read the dream to me, and I told her, "Okay. First of all, this woman experienced a sexual trauma, and now she's afraid of strangers." My mother asked, "How do you know all this?" I told her I just knew it. I sort of felt it. I don't know where I got this ability.

I write whenever I'm bored. I've been writing for as long as I can remember. Recently I wrote a poem about a friend who was killed in a car accident. We had met through mutual friends, and we connected. He became my big brother. I felt great being with him. I showed the poem to his parents and friends, and I made it into a song. The poem is now available on a creative writing site on the Internet.

When I write a story, I don't know what the ending will be. Sometimes there's a surprise ending, and sometimes not. Whatever goes! One of my favorite stories is about two kids—myself and an imaginary friend—walking on train tracks and encountering strange things. It's snowing on an April morning around five AM. We meet a talking pink lion, and continue walking. We enter a train station with pictures on the wall. A train arrives, and suddenly we start shrinking. I open the door of the train, and then I really see who I am. The moral of my story is that if at five o'clock in the morning you go to a train station and see a pink lion talking for no reason, keep on walking in order to get in touch with yourself.

I believe in a superior force, but I don't believe in God. If there were a God, I wouldn't be here, because I don't observe the Sabbath. I have all types of friends, some religious and some not, and even some who are observant but don't believe in the existence of God. As far as I'm concerned, until I see God, I'll not wake up from my dream, which I call reality. Anyway, I don't have strong faith. I believe everyone is their own God. Everyone has to make decisions for themselves. Everyone is in charge of their own destiny.

I have a boyfriend. I met him about four months ago, but I've only known him well for two months. He's cute and smart, and he likes to have a good time. We always go to parties together, where we enjoy sitting and talking. The last time we met he told me he loved me. Then he asked me how I felt. I said that I didn't know what love is and that I didn't know whether or not I loved him.

The important thing in a relationship like mine with my boyfriend is honesty. We should have a good time and not be pressured to do anything we don't want to do. I have female friends who have fights with their boyfriends, and I observe how they reconcile. But I haven't learned too much from observing them, because I'm only fifteen, and I don't understand life that well.

There are "red lights" in a relationship, but the limits are not that clear to me. The bottom line is that I haven't asked my boyfriend to do anything he wouldn't want to do, and he hasn't asked me to do anything I wouldn't want to do. I have a girlfriend whose boyfriend is much older than she is. That won't happen to me. I won't have a relationship with anyone two years older or more, because I know he'll be looking for things I don't care about. I'm not saying that it can't work out, but to me it's just not the right kind of relationship.

My boyfriend is right-wing. Even though I'm on the left, he tells me that I'll become right-wing. I answer, "Yes, whatever you say." He doesn't want to change his political views, even though he's an important part of my life. But I cannot control him, and he cannot control me.

In my school, most of the students are right-wing. But I was educated by my parents to favor the left, and I agree with the way I was raised. Since 1948 we've had a state, and we have the right to live here. But we should forget any connection between the land and God or the Torah. Later we conquered territories, and then returned some. I think

"What I want is for there to be no hatred any longer and for everyone to enjoy themselves."

we really don't need these territories. How many families do we have in the settlements? It's absurd that we have more soldiers guarding settlers than the number of settlers themselves. People should not endanger their lives just so that others can live on a piece of land which some other people believe has been given to them by God.

The Palestinians demand a homeland. They want a place to live. We were also that way once. We did not have a state, a home, a place to return to. Now we have our home. Brothers of the Palestinians didn't accept them in other Arab countries. They should have. It's not as if they don't have space. But we Jews didn't settle the whole land. And that was a good thing. Giving up even one square meter helps the Palestinians. But the settlers say, "You're asking us to evacuate a whole city." Actually the settlers don't occupy that many whole cities. They have ten families here and forty there. They should give these settlements up and leave.

I'd be ready to leave my own house if that would give us peace and quiet. Of course I would! My mother doesn't allow me to ride on buses because of the suicide bombings. I wish I could do something to bring calm to the region. It's okay for Palestinians to live here in Jerusalem. Let them be a majority, let there be a Palestinian mayor, but bring calm to us. We want to go to sleep knowing that there are no soldiers guarding checkpoints and endangering their lives in Gaza.

What I want is for there to be no hatred any longer and for everyone to enjoy themselves. My father has been going to a restaurant in Abu-Ghosh for a long time. The people in that town know him well, and they're great.

I don't understand why suicide bombers kill themselves. If you want a state, you should *live* for it. If you *die* for it, how will that help? I understand that the bombers are trying to express their pain. And that some are trying to express their hatred for Israel and are willing to kill innocent people. There are no Jewish terrorists. If we stoop to that level, we need to stop ourselves.

I think we need to speak with the Palestinians, a conversation that is eye to eye, without a security force present. You have to consult people about what they want. Israelis must talk to Palestinians and find out what they want and try to develop strong connections. I once had an opportunity to speak with a Palestinian, but not one from the Territories. Once a group of us had a meeting with Palestinians. I didn't speak with them personally, but others did. My hope is that we can live together, with no separation. For me, security has to do with being careful when you're walking late at night or catching a taxi by yourself. When there is peace, we can walk together in the street, and Israelis will not say, "Palestinians, Yuk!" I don't think there needs to be separation between us. The idea that Jews and Arabs can't live together is deeply embedded in us.

I know a little Arabic, but not enough to hold a conversation. I'm studying Arabic in school. I think it's important. Why should Palestinians have to study Hebrew when we don't have to study Arabic? If people don't want to study Arabic, it's their problem. Knowing Arabic will help me throughout life. If you go to a place where they speak Arabic and you're not able to understand what's going on, you'll be lost. This happened to me in various places. It's nice when you meet an Arab, and you can tell him, "*Shokran.*" They're happy you know Arabic.

Many Jews feel that they are above it all. Once we were assimilated in other countries and didn't have a land of our own. Then World War II broke out and Hitler arose. We all know the rest. But there's a difference between then and now. It seems preferable to me now to live in a land together with the Palestinians.

I myself feel Jewish. I feel it on holidays, when I'm observing traditions, and in many other ways. Here things related to being Jewish are taken for granted. It's expressed daily. It's no big deal. It's not even so important to me that my children marry someone Jewish. If our situation in Israel worsens, it will be less important to me to maintain Jewish identity in the family. If the situation improves, however, then I'd be very proud that we're Jews.

CHAPTER 18

KHAEL

"I hope there'll be peace between Israelis and Palestinians. We need to live with each other without problems and without some being masters and some servants."

My name is Khael. I live in Birzeit, Palestine. I'm fifteen years old. My family consists of my parents, three brothers, and twin sisters. I'm about to be promoted to tenth grade at Ibrahimiya School in Ramallah.

My twin sisters are older than I am. They're already in college. When they get discouraged about all the work they have to do in college, they come and talk with me about the subjects they're studying. This makes me happy. I feel like I'm a helpful human being in the family. I feel the same when my brother consults me about his problems. Although it's not in my nature to make trouble, problems sometimes arise between me and my friends. When my sisters hear about the problem, they immediately come to me and try to calm me down.

My father is very understanding. He gives us the freedom to make our own decisions. Once I told him that I wanted to become a priest. My father didn't interfere. He just warned me not to make such a decision too quickly.

Birzeit is a beautiful town. Those of us who live in Birzeit have close ties with our neighbors. But it's not like it used to be in the past—not like it was in the time of my grandmothers. Even relationships among relatives are supposedly not as close as they once were. Our life is much more difficult now.

This is my first year in Ibrahimiya School. Things are different from the way they were in my junior high school, but I'm getting used to how things are here. By now the other students have begun chatting with me, and I have four very good friends. We confide in one another. Sometimes there are misunderstandings among us, but we forgive each other pretty quickly. Friendship is a treasure that can be yours for life.

It's my nature to joke around. I like having a soul full of commotion, and I like making people laugh. Making others laugh makes me laugh in turn. Sometimes my joking around involves lying. I think there's no human being alive who doesn't lie. I know that lying isn't a good thing to do. I know it can cause harm. But when I lie, it's just a way of introducing something humorous into a conversation.

I write in both Arabic and English. I'd like to learn Hebrew better so that I can know how to deal with the Israeli Occupation. I especially need to be able to express myself to Israeli soldiers at the checkpoints. That way I can defend myself.

Before the Occupation a trip from Birzeit to Ramallah, where I go to school, would be an easy, lovely ride. But now it's not the case. Yesterday a barrier was erected, and we were late to school. There were patrols of Israeli soldiers who set up inspection points for no reason— only to harass and delay people. We got out of the car and talked with the soldier in charge. The soldier said, "If you don't go back now, I'll begin shooting." We went back to the taxi and waited for an hour. There was heavy traffic at that time. Now I regret that I left my old school in Birzeit. Israeli soldiers don't treat me like a human being. They take pity on animals more than they do on us.

I hope there'll be peace between Israelis and Palestinians. We need to live with each other without problems and without some being masters and some servants. I hope that Israelis understand how much Palestinians suffer from the Occupation. My dream is that I'll be able to visit my uncles who live within Israel. Right now we only talk with them by telephone.

If I were to suddenly become rich, I'd pay off all my family's debts and finish work on our house. Then I'd buy things for the family and also help the Palestinian people. If I had any money left over, I'd invent a way to travel that can't do any harm to anyone. A plane would not be a good idea, because it could fall. A ship might sink. Trains might crash into each other. I'd invent a vehicle that could never do any harm. There's already too much harm being done to people all around me.

CHAPTER 19

NOFAR

"I am really not
like my sister.
We like
different things.
I don't listen to
a lot of music.
When she
puts on music,
I scream."

I'm Nofar Vaknin, a thirteen-year-old girl living in Shoham, a small town in central Israel. I have a twin sister and a sixteen-year-old brother. My mother teaches kindergarten, and my father works in the police. Both my parents understand me, but my father understands me better. My mother is busier with her own things.

I'm really not like my sister, not even physically. We're not identical at all. We like different things. For example, I don't listen to a lot of music, and she does. When she puts on music, I scream. She's more involved with her studies, while I'm more interested in socializing. I like people who want to have a good time. There are things that I'm good at, and there are things my sister is good at. I'm very much into matching my clothing. She's very smart, gifted in math. She gets perfect grades all the time.

My brother and I used to have a bad relationship. He and I were always fighting. Now he helps me a lot, and we get along very well. Despite the ups and downs in my relationships with my family, the bottom line is that I love them all. I hope my parents, brother, and sister will live for many years.

Three years ago I moved to Shoham from Tel Aviv. In Shoham people are very nice. They help one other. My neighbors are really good-hearted. In Tel Aviv it seemed that everyone worried about himself.

Every change is a good one, but truthfully, here in Shoham I'm not managing so well in my new school. I'm having a hard time adjusting to my classes. I know that it'll work out, though.

In Tel Aviv the kids were cooler than in Shoham. Boys here can be cruel. Although I have many girl friends—thirty-two of them—I don't get along well with boys. They don't try to help me or anything like that. They only bother me. Boys stole my cell phone. But maybe it's not just in Shoham that kids are cruel. Maybe it's because I'm now in junior

"I like to bake cakes. However, often when I'm working with eggs I break them. My mother says eggs are not my thing."

high school. Teachers help you less in junior high school than they do in elementary school. You need to manage relationships with others by yourself. I'm only in my first year in junior high, so maybe it will be easier for me in the coming years.

I'm very interested in art. I draw very nicely. I was accepted into the art track in school at Shoham, with exhibitions and all. This is an area I'm really involved in. My father says I have a very successful future in art. He tells everyone that his daughter will be an artist someday. But I feel insecure about my drawing. I don't see my being good at art as something special. Maybe I don't appreciate myself enough.

I'm sensitive to everything that happens to me. I get hurt very easily. I would say that this is my biggest problem. Every time I say this, my father tells me that there are people with bigger problems. I'm always walking around with the feeling that my problem is the biggest. Once I saw a woman who could not use her legs. Now that's a real problem. My situation is obviously not as severe as this, but every person thinks that his problem is the most important. Little by little you come to see that there are people with bigger problems. My father says that there are people who would want to change places with me as I am now. Truthfully, my parents give me whatever I want, and I really do not have any major problems.

I have a special liking for dogs. I once had a small dog named Shelly. She was really cute. At the time that I had Shelly, we lived in a house. When we moved to an apartment, it became more difficult to keep her, so we gave her to my great-aunt. It was so hard to give her up, and it was hard for the dog to leave us. When we left her in my great-aunt's house, she walked right back toward us as we were driving away.

I like to bake cakes. However, often when I'm working with eggs I break them. This morning I put eggs on the counter, and they rolled off and fell. Yesterday I left them in the refrigerator, one on top of the other, and they all broke. Six eggs dropped. My mother says eggs are not my thing.

The conflict with the Palestinians is scary. Our situation is horrible with all the attacks. My parents don't allow me to go to certain places because of the danger. But at this moment in time it's safer. I'm not that connected to politics. If it is necessary to go to war, then I would be really stressed, I would be in shock, and I would be scared that something will happen to me. I think that Shoham is more secure than Tel Aviv. Tel Aviv has had attacks. I have not seen anything in Shoham. But security forces are everywhere, and you are still checked wherever you go.

I think the way the conflict can be resolved is that we have to turn to the people in the settlements. I think it's the settlers who prevent peace from coming. Settlers are going to get money for leaving, and they should buy apartments for themselves. It's worthwhile to help them, because the attacks hurt everyone. I can tell you that I can understand each side's position. It's hard for the people in the settlements to leave. I understand that everyone has a house, and he is connected to it emotionally and all, but I also understand that the settlers will be compensated. For all the problems we have in Israel, there are countries that are worse than mine. Israel is a relatively normal place in comparison to other places.

I would like to meet Palestinian children and to see how they cope with the conflict. I'd like to see the differences between the ways they live and the way I live. In the same way, I don't exactly know how Africans or Americans live. It interests me a lot to meet different people and to be exposed to many cultures.

My dreams for the future? I think I want to go into the field of medicine. I think about pediatrics. There's always a need for it, and I love children, little ones especially. I hope that only good things will happen to me and that I'll have enough money and get through life easily. I want people to accept me. That's important to me.

CHAPTER 20

MURAD

"Any war which aims to occupy other people is wrong."

My name is Murad. I was born in 1992, and I live with my parents, a sister, and two brothers. We live in Abu-Ghosh, near Jerusalem, and I attend Abu-Ghosh School, where I've just finished sixth grade.

I'm the oldest of the three sons. Sometimes I don't enjoy being the eldest brother. Every time something happens my parents say, "You're the big one, they're only small." I realize that my brothers will always be younger than I am, even when they're bigger. When I buy things for myself, it seems that my younger brothers always want them. They go to my father and start crying. My father then tells me to share whatever I have with them. So it seems that in a family the eldest brother is oppressed. When I become a father, I won't allow this to happen. The kind of rules I'll make will depend on how a child behaves.

One time, when I was very young, I felt really misunderstood by my mother. I learned that an egg needs warmth in order to hatch, so I hid an egg under the cover of my bed. Then I went to school. When I came back, I found the egg smashed inside the bed. I asked my mother, "Was a chicken hatched?" "No," replied my mother, "there's only a stink."

Our neighborhood in Abu-Ghosh is beautiful and not so crowded, but there are no playgrounds for us to play in. We play in the street after school because we're not allowed to use the school playground. But some kids don't follow the rules. These boys jump over the wall of the school in order to enter the playground.

We play many different games depending on the weather. Everyone in the neighborhood is my friend. When I want to play, I just go outside to meet them. I've never argued with my friends, but I see them arguing with each other. When I observe that they've stopped talking to each other, I ask them why. Then I become the mediator. Sometimes I feel I even have to lie in order to help them reconcile. Usually lying is not a good idea, but I don't feel guilty when I lie in this way, because it's a lie told for good reason.

At school, when two boys get angry and stop speaking with each other, the class divides into two groups, each supporting one of the boys. Then they start calling each other funny names, like "giraffe mouse" and *fakusa* (a kind of cucumber).

My favorite subjects are science, math, and English. But when we get too much homework I'm turned off to school. When I do homework in my house, I feel as if I'm still at school. However, I feel I have to finish school because it may lead me to a good job.

In third grade we took an intelligence test. The fifteen students who performed the best on this test were tested a second time in order to see

**"Sometimes I don't enjoy being the eldest brother.
Every time something happens, my parents say,
'You're the big one, they're only small.' So it seems that
in a family the eldest brother is oppressed."**

if they were qualified for entrance into a Gifted Children's Program. I passed the second test. All of us in this program studied chemistry and physics and performed lots of experiments. Hebrew is the language of instruction. In the first year they brought in a translator, but now we can understand Hebrew on our own. There are very few Arab students in this program.

Although I speak Hebrew, I shy away from interacting with Israeli students. In the breaks at school, I sit alone. Sometimes I can't understand what they're saying in Hebrew. The kids don't speak with me. If there's someone in my group from Abu-Ghosh, I'll chat with him during the breaks.

I don't like Prime Minister Sharon. Before him, the prime minister was Barak. The situation between Palestinians and Israelis was better then. The two peoples were more integrated. Barak allowed people from the West Bank who have orange identity cards to enter Jerusalem.

But Sharon came and put checkpoints everywhere. At the checkpoint in Ramallah there's a path for cars and a path for pedestrians. Everyone who passes has to be checked, and they inspect everyone's identity card. This makes people's lives difficult. Palestinians started the Intifada because of the policies of the Israeli government. Sharon controls the whole state. His government is building a very high wall to separate people from one another.

Any war that aims to occupy other people is wrong. There's a lot of land. It's possible to live in this land without war. However, if there's a war against the Occupation, it's an OK war. I want to advance the peace process between Israel and Palestine because every day I hear about explosions, and I know that Palestinian people die.

If I were to get rich, I would contribute part of my money to institutions that work for peace. I'd also give some to poor people and the rest to improve my home and help my friends. In the future, I'd like to become a humble surgeon—an ordinary man who has a job.

CHAPTER 21

RAVID

"I really want for us to become more patient, we need to stop our offensive behavior, and become more self-reflective."

My name is Ravid Tachman. I attend the ORT school in Nazareth Elit in northern Israel. I'm going into the eleventh grade. My father, David, and my mom, Carmela, are in their forties. My brother is in fourth grade, and my sister is in seventh grade. We all get along pretty well. My brother and I get along the best. With my sister there are occasional conflicts, but the situation is really OK.

In addition to my studies at school, I've been playing clarinet for nine years, piano for five years, and guitar for the last six months. During my elementary school years, I attended a music school. At this school they test you when you enter third grade in order to see what instrument would be best for you to play. You have to practice every day in order to reach a certain level of expertise. I can't always find the time to practice as much as I should, but somehow things work out. I plan to take my *bagrut* examinations in music. At this point I don't see myself as a professional musician in the future. It's just a fun thing for me to be doing.

I watch a TV program called *Exit.* My friends and I disagree with many other Israelis who think the program is vulgar. If someone doesn't like a program, let him not watch it. It would be inappropriate to censor it. I think the program speaks to the youth of our country. The themes of the show are provocative. If what they're saying doesn't get to us on TV, we'll find it on the Internet or in conversations on the street. There's no censorship on the street!

I'm a counselor in the Labor and Study Youth Movement. The movement has thousands of trainees. I've been in it for three years, and personally I love it. It's something special when you're part of a group. When we traveled to the Rabin rally, I felt like I was really part of something larger than me. I looked around me and saw so many others wearing the blue shirts of our movement. It was a moving experience.

I ask myself why I was drawn to the movement in the first place. There was a counselor last year who really had an influence on me. It was just plain fun to have her lead us in activities. At that time our activities were not connected to politics. They were mainly social. We discussed what's happening in Israeli society and things like that. But this year we had an explosive argument about the political situation. All of us needed to step outside and calm down. The others did not agree with what I had to say. It sounded strange to them.

Even though I enjoy being in the movement, my political opinions differ from pretty much everyone else's views. I'm really alone in this way. Most of the others who belong to the Labor Movement are leftists. That means you give up more and more land, and I don't believe that's right. I think the political situation is very complicated. I don't believe we should kill Palestinians. That would be wrong, especially since we are a people that suffered the Holocaust. Yet nothing that we do seems to satisfy the Palestinians. Every time we do something, nothing changes for the better. It seems like there will always be bombings. We say we want to leave the Territories, and they still say they will not stop the attacks. So, it's unrealistic to think we'll have peace soon. Everyone on the outside seems to think that if only we Israelis relent, peace will come easily. They don't realize that it's just not that simple. Everything we do has to be agreed upon by both parties. But the Palestinians want everything or nothing, which makes for an impossible situation.

I don't see the significance of all the protests against the government. If the prime minister decides to withdraw from the Territories, allows the Palestinians to create a state, and decides on specific borders, then the situation will change—as long as there aren't protests. There's no other way. Jews have been here since the creation of the state. We have to help create a state for the Palestinians, just as we created one for Jews. We should not depend on a fence or on a border patrol striking them every time they need to bring merchandise across a border or come to a hospital. These people don't have a life.

Their house is not a home. They're always afraid that soldiers will come and blow up their houses. This is the kind of thing that was done to us during the Holocaust. So what are we, the same as those who carried out crimes during the Holocaust? It's clear to me that the Palestinians have a reason to come here and attack us. Yet, we are a state and all of us—not just the government—are responsible for our policies.

When we decide on a response following an attack, we should not just impose a curfew and limit their resources. We just need to restrict them in some way. They're looking for a state the same way we looked for a state—only we looked for it in a more normal way.

However, I have to say that fear of bombings does not have a great effect on me. This is my country, and if I'm afraid to walk around it, why should anyone else want to come here? The situation is screwed up, that's true. There's nothing much else to say about it. I know that my friends are not afraid of the situation either. Even in large crowds, like those at the festivals, I rely on security to protect me. Fear of attacks does not prevent me from attending these events. If I'm fated to be there when there's an attack, then that's how it is. I'm not afraid.

Being on the left with regard to the conflict is not all that my movement stands for. The movement emphasizes social equality. That's something I'm very connected to. I participate in Labor Youth activities that I hope will help bring about greater equality within Israel. There was a protest by the Labor Youth Movement a year ago against the reforms of the minister of finance. He reduced the budget for the handicapped, the elderly, and the sick. No money was taken away from the ultra-orthodox religious parties, something that bothered me a lot. He also did not touch the rich. There's a huge gap between those who have money in our society and those who don't.

There are many Palestinians living here in my city—too many. But that's also the uniqueness of the city. It was created to avoid discrimination. I don't blame Palestinians for living here. It's their right to live wherever they want. They have Israeli citizenship. It's our fault that so many are here, because we sell them things they need. If it were very important not to have Palestinians in this city, we would stop selling them these things. However, when you actually see money, it's a different thing altogether.

I have to say that walking around with a bunch of girls on Friday night is not the safest thing in the world. The Palestinians come down here from Nazareth or other villages and simply enjoy scaring young women and girls. This can even happen in the movie theaters, where there are lots of people. That won't stop them. Most of the younger Jewish people who used to live in Nazareth Elit have left. They work here and continue to shop here, but that's it. They won't consider living here for only one reason: Palestinians are here. There was a family who lived near us and who left just because Palestinians lived here. It's ironic: Their source of employment is here, and they're here all day, but they live in places like Solelim, Shimshit, and Kibbutz Yfaat. There's even something humorous about the situation. Something bothers you about a place, but you don't stop coming to it. It's retarded. I'm upset because I know my family won't ever leave. Here's where they earn their living.

After the army, I won't commit to saying that I will not leave for Tel Aviv. But then I think: What will become of the Land of Israel? Will it consist only of Tel Aviv? All the young people say that after the army they'll rent an apartment in Tel Aviv, work there, and study at the university. But that doesn't happen in more than 50 percent of the cases. What I think will probably happen is that I'll rent an apartment here in my hometown. I don't care which neighborhood or which street. Personally I really love this city, despite the fact that there aren't too many hangout places for young people without a driver's license. If someone wants to do something, he can really do it here in Nazareth Elit. The people you're with are more important than the place you live in. My friends are important to me, and I prefer to be wherever they are.

If I do wind up staying here, I'll want to participate in the life of the city. I want to help improve the life of the people here. I see what my sister and others her age are going through. Every grade level in the schools is becoming progressively more vulgar and aggressive. I see this happening in my own school as well. In my grade level, people started to smoke at the end of ninth grade. The younger crowd starts smoking at the end of eighth grade. And these youngsters don't join youth movements— and they don't even ask themselves whether they should or shouldn't.

To conclude, I really want for us Israelis to become more patient. We need to stop our offensive behavior, become less stressed out and more self-reflective.

CHAPTER 22
REEM

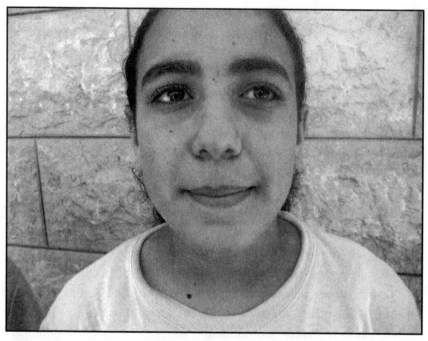

"If I were to become the head of the municipality,
I'd make the dreams of the children come true.
I'd build playgrounds and install pools."

My name is Reem. I live in Yama. There are seven of us in the family. I have three sisters and one brother. My mother is a schoolteacher, and my father is a businessman.

I study at the Al-Zahra School where I'll be entering seventh grade. I like studying math, but what I love most is grammar. Parsing sentences is like a hobby. When I'm parsing a sentence, I feel as if I'm eating a plate of *mulukhiyah*, my favorite food.

I'm not fond of some of my teachers, like the one who teaches us geography. I don't like geography. It's a bore. The teacher comes to class, sits on the chair, and says, "Open the book and answer the questions." In class we just repeat all the things we've studied in our textbooks. There's a handicapped girl in the class whose aunt accompanies her to school each day. The teacher spends most of the class talking with the girl's aunt. But we can't tell the headmaster about this because the teacher is married to the principal's sister.

Not all teachers are like my geography teacher. My Arabic teacher is committed to improving the intellectual skills of all the students in the class. And our English teacher is young. We feel she's our age. She explains things so well that we feel we really understand what's being taught in class.

When I see a person in the street who speaks a language I know, I feel I must go and speak with him or her and respond to any request for help. I really want to understand what he or she is saying. I love studying languages. I'm currently studying Arabic, English, and Hebrew.

One time our teacher assigned us the task of designing a science project. Three girls and I decided to work on this project together. Both girls came to my house a total of four times in order to complete this assignment, but instead of doing our work, we mainly spent our time chatting and playing. We only spent half an hour doing our work. When we saw the projects that other groups had completed, we realized how much better their work was than ours. So we decided to do the project over again. This time we worked for more than six hours. The project turned out beautiful, and we received an excellent grade.

I like reading. I especially enjoy fiction. The last story I read was by a Palestinian author. The title of the story was "Talea Sayf." It described the daily lives of the main characters, emphasizing how impatiently they all wait for the summer when they can do all the things they've been wanting to do all year.

I've been playing the piano for one year. Two of my classmates play very well, and I had hoped to learn how to play piano the way they do. I begged and begged my parents to allow me to take piano lessons until they agreed. My father bought the instrument, and my mother drove me to my lessons. I adore folk music.

There's a lot of joy in our family life. I feel happy when I'm together with my sisters chatting about this and that—about friends, and even about household tasks. We also talk about the television series we're currently watching. We all make predictions about how the shows will

"Friendship to me is like living in a steady stream of sincerity, honesty, love, and cooperation flowing from one person to another."

end. Another thing we do is read stories in English, competing with one another to see who'll finish first. A typical evening: We tidy the house, eat dinner, and do our homework. Then we watch television.

My sisters and I do have our problems, but most arise from disputes over trivial matters—about things like who gets to wear certain clothes or certain shoes. My older sister guards her possessions carefully. She likes us to give her things, but she doesn't like to give us her things in return. Sometimes I tease my sisters. When my father gets angry with them, I sit and imitate him and my sisters' reactions.

My parents stress the importance of reading books, something I'm in full agreement with. We have to go to sleep at a fixed hour, and they put limits on how much time we can spend watching television. Sometimes I have to interrupt a television show I'm watching because we have visitors and I'm told by my mother to go and make tea or coffee. One time I wanted to attend my friend's birthday party. But my father and mother both said no, because there were problems in the girl's family. I basically agree with the way my parents are raising me. They're giving me the guidance I need. When I get married, I'll follow their philosophy of child rearing. However, even though it's important to obey parents, I think I'll ease up a bit on all the restrictions.

We live in a neighborhood where houses are located very close to one together. All the homes have orange and fig trees in the yards. Our neighbors are my relatives. They're my uncles. I play in the courtyard with my cousins, both girls and boys. We race our bikes and play marbles. Our village doesn't have playgrounds or parks. There's just no money in our municipal budget for parks. We have to go to the Jewish towns if we want to play in places like these. If I were to become the head of the municipality, I'd make the dreams of the children come true. I'd build playgrounds, fix up yards, install pools—provide everything that children like. But I do like living in our neighborhood, because we don't need to use a car when we want to visit our uncles. We can just walk.

Friendship to me is like living in a steady stream of sincerity, honesty, love, and cooperation flowing from one person to another. I have a really good friend. When you look at her face, you see a lot of love there. She's been my friend since we were very small. At school we both use the same kinds of pens. One time, we forgot our pens at home. When we arrived at school that day, we found a pen under the desk. I said, "This is *my* pen," and she said, "This is *my* pen." We were so angry that we stopped talking to one another. At the end of that day another girl came and asked if we had seen the pen she had lost. So it turned out that the pen we were fighting about was neither mine nor hers. When we got home, we found our pens. We could do nothing but laugh.

I'm a Muslim. Islam is a set of principles and beliefs that you must put into practice. Some people say that all of the problems facing the world at present are connected to Muslims. This is simply not true. If there's one bad apple, that doesn't mean that all of the apples are bad. For instance, in the Vietnam War, Americans killed many innocent people in Vietnam. Does this mean that all Americans are bad? No!

I believe in heaven and hell, because they are mentioned in the Quran. I try to follow all the principles of Islam out of love, not from fear of punishment. I wear the veil because I love following Allah's commands. The Prophet Muhammad, may peace be upon him, always used to pray at midnight. His daughter Fatimah asked him: "Oh messenger of Allah, why do you pray at midnight? Is it because you wish to be rewarded in paradise?" The Prophet replied, "I follow the principles of Islam just because I love Allah, not because I fear him. I have to be a thankful slave." Allah is ever merciful and all-forgiving. This means if I do something bad and then repent, Allah will forgive me.

My way of being religious is different from my grandmother's way. For example, when my grandmother covers her hair, half is left exposed, and when she prays she doesn't pray with reverence. She looks around, to the right and to the left. I try to concentrate on what I'm saying when I pray.

I like to go to the mall to shop. But the problem is that the only mall near us is located in Hadera, a Jewish town. When I'm there, I'm not comfortable. Everyone looks at me in a certain way, as if I were an unacceptable person. I'm just treated differently from Jewish people.

Although the Israeli prime minister is guilty of killing Palestinian children and women, I do not support killing Israelis. The problem between Israel and Palestine is the Israeli Occupation. As for the Palestinian leadership, I will say it is a failure. The Palestinian people are dying, and the leadership hasn't done anything to help the situation.

If I were to become the head of the Israeli government, the first thing I would do is make peace, because that's what's necessary to put an end to all the problems of the inhabitants of the land. War is something terrible. Peace is rest, satisfaction—a white bird spreading love among people. It's purity itself.

When I think about my future, I know I'll live with my family until I marry. I want my husband to be wealthy and handsome. I'd like him to have a college degree, own his own business, and be religious. I also know that I want to go to college. I'd like to be like my uncle, a college professor. And I'd like to study in America. Perhaps someday I'll teach in Tel Aviv University.

CHAPTER 23
SHANY

"My dreams for the future include finding someone
who will love me and whom I'll love in return.
But first of all I've got to be OK within myself."

My name is Shany, which means red, like the color red. I love my name. I was born in Ramat Hasharon, but now I live in Ramot Hashavim, near Kfar Saba. I have twin brothers who are older than I am. They're twenty-two. As the youngest child, I'm the spoiled one in the family, a role that I enjoy. When my brothers and I were young, we fought a lot about my parents giving me things that they didn't give them.

Mother is a lawyer working in a family firm. My father is a financial adviser. My parents separated when I was six years old and now they're divorced. I live with Mother. My father lives in Ramat Hasharon. We have a good relationship with one another. The divorce—like all divorces—created problems for me, but all in all I came out OK, not terrible!

We have a good relationship with our neighbors. But I have to say we don't know everyone very well. There's one neighbor who just drops in if she's passing by. She says, "Hi," and my mother invites her in for coffee. Although my mother is busy in the law firm, she makes sure she has time for these kinds of visits.

There are certain times when I feel especially close to the family. I'm really happy when we're all together at important events, like birthdays. At those times we can be as many as twenty or so people celebrating in one place.

My mother has established certain rules in our family. Mom tells us that when we're at home, we should use the regular phone, not the cell phone. But I would only use the phone for a minute's conversation. When I get married, I'll raise my children pretty much the same way my parents have raised me. I think I was brought up with good values, and I'll pass those on. I think the best thing I learned from my parents was to respect everyone, no matter who that person is—regardless of their age, religion, or culture.

I don't like to lie. But there are times I have lied. I've lied to my teachers in school. These lies were always about minor things, like about not doing my homework.

I've just finished high school in Kfar Saba. In the beginning I had a bit of a hard time, but in the end I can say that I really enjoyed my time at school. I liked being with the other students. And there was one teacher who had the kind of personal touch that was special. She remembered everything you said, even the smallest detail. And she related to us with a sense of humor.

Most of my good friends are female. It's more comfortable to be friends with girls. And just in terms of numbers, there were always more girls than boys in my class.

I actually wanted to drop out in the beginning of the eleventh grade. We took a math test and I failed it. This was the first time in all my years in school that I failed an exam. The teacher returned the tests, and everyone saw that I had failed. I said nothing about it, but they started to clap their hands and shout, "Shany, congratulations on your first failure." All I wanted was to be left alone. At that moment I wanted to get up and leave school.

We're allowed to choose two main subjects to study in school. I chose film and chemistry. But after about one lesson in chemistry I understood that it wasn't for me. I told those in charge at school that I wanted to drop chemistry. They tried to convince me to stay with chemistry, and they insisted on checking with my parents that it was OK for me drop it. Finally, I succeeded in staying with my film studies alone.

When you study film, you have to make two short films, ten to twelve minutes in length. I was involved with two such films—one that I actually filmed and one that I edited. The one I edited was about a female who was in love with her girlfriend. She was uncertain whether or not she was truly in love with that person. It turns out that she was deeply in love with her, and she had to struggle within herself about how to tell her girlfriend how she felt. The story ended with her writing about her feelings in her diary. Later her girlfriend saw what was written in the diary.

Working on this project was a good experience. It was an important topic to deal with. I should mention that this story was written by a female friend of mine. She wrote this story because she recognized some of these tendencies in her girlfriend.

The movie I filmed myself turned out to be a comedy about

someone who is sure that rabbits want to control the world. She then tries to convince everyone to kill all rabbits everywhere they can be found, so that they would not be able to take over the earth. My girlfriend had the idea for this one also. It was really a really funny movie.

When I think about the future, I hope I'll continue with my film studies. First, however, I'll need to go into the army. I assume that if I really had a choice in the matter, I might prefer not to go. But I believe that being in the army matures you, so it's OK for two years. Two years is a lot, but it's a period that helps you experience all sorts of things.

My dreams for the future include finding someone who will love me and whom I'll love in return. But first of all I know I have to be OK within myself. Once I've found my love, I dream about living in a place where there's some peace and stability, a place where I can raise a family. I also dream about becoming involved with work that really interests me, a profession that will be good for me in many ways. At this moment it's film, but maybe that will change. I'm not certain. When I was young, I thought that I'd go to work in the family law firm, but now it doesn't look that way to me. My mother encourages me to do whatever I want to do.

I believe there's a God, but my belief is not very strong. I don't know if God is male or female, although in the Bible it's written that God is male. Sometimes it bothers me that God is thought of as male, but I'm not all that disturbed by this. I'm not one of those feminists who are only for women. I can relate to God as a male. But I have to say that if God exists, I hope he doesn't live in any one place. I hope he travels around the world all the time. If there's a God, there are lots of things he needs to do in our world.

I think a lot about what happens when people die. Perhaps it's the case that good people die young because they're needed somewhere else. I can't say that I know anything with certainty about all this. I think less about where I might have been before I was born. But I do care about the matter of where I came from, and I'm always trying to get a grasp on this matter.

When I have free time, I usually go to the mall. I've had my car for

**"If God exists, I hope he doesn't live in any one place.
I hope he travels around the world all the time.
There are lots of things he needs to do in our world."**

only a few months, but I received a parking ticket the first time I drove
to school. I couldn't understand why this happened. Then I noticed a
sign saying that you can park only until two o'clock. I said, "Wow," and
called my mother to tell her what had happened. She said that I hadn't
done such a terrible thing, that what happened to me could happen to
anyone. I understand that the law is the law, and I respect that.

However, there are laws in Israel that I'm more in agreement with
and some that I agree with less. One law I definitely don't agree with is
the citizenship law, which I studied about in school. Israel annexed East
Jerusalem and gave her residents only residency, not citizenship. This is
a racist law. I try to tell this to everyone. The law resembles the Nazi citizenship laws during the 1930s. How can we do to someone else what we
don't want to have happen to us? The people I talk with about this say,
"Yes, but listen. We have to protect the Jewish State." I then ask them to

explain what that really means. I cannot change this law myself, but I can work with others to change it by putting pressure on the government.

When Ariel Sharon became prime minister, I thought he would be worse than he is. The mere fact that he is beginning to think about pullbacks and evacuations of the settlement—the fact that these things are in his head—is a pleasant surprise to me. I think that if we are to move forward in the peace process, the government needs to decide to pull out of all the settlements. On the Palestinian side, I believe that Arafat has some control. He needs to make an effort to stop the attacks. And as for what ordinary people can do, I think that most people are not trying to do more than they're already doing, and I can understand why. First of all you want everything to be okay, and at this point in time, it's hard to achieve this.

I'm ready to divide the land into Israel and Palestine so that there can be peace. I think that we're not coming close to achieving this because everyone expects the other side to give in. Each side is acting out of a kind of sense of self-respect. If we don't succeed in achieving a stable peace, I'll want to move to the United States or Australia. I met an American friend on the Internet, and I'd love to go visit her. She'd also like to visit me. We did meet in person once—in the United States a year ago. We were together for a whole week, and we had a great time.

CHAPTER 24

ROLLA

"When I need to talk about problems,
I prefer talking with boys.
There's no jealousy among boys."

My name is Rolla. I'm eighteen years old, and I live in Haifa. We're five in our family, three sisters and my parents. I'm the middle sister. My older sister is twenty-one. She studies at Tel Aviv University. My younger sister is thirteen.

Sometimes there's some tension in the atmosphere at home. I'm moody, and little things make me tense. But there aren't any real problems in the household. We enjoy being with one another, especially when we're traveling somewhere together. But I feel close to my family even when we're doing ordinary things, like going shopping or just sitting around and chatting. And whenever I have problems with friends or teachers at school, my family is right there to help me.

In general, my sisters and I don't have to follow many rules at home. One thing we're not allowed to do is use the cell phone. My father says it gives off harmful rays. I'm only allowed to use it in emergency circumstances. When I have my own family, I'll insist that there be many more restrictions in the household. For example, my little sister uses the Internet late at night whenever she wants. I feel that's not appropriate, and I won't allow my daughter to do it.

My neighborhood is in the middle of Haifa, near markets and restaurants. We have beautiful views of the Mediterranean and the port of Haifa. Some of the residents are very nice, very cultured. But our block is always dirty. There are some people who are just not considerate. They don't care about the environment, and they don't respect the need for quiet at night. Sometimes we hear loud music late at night. You wouldn't want to have these people for your neighbors.

I've just completed my high school studies at Rahat Al-Nasra in Haifa. My favorite subjects were physics and math. History turned me off because I don't like having to memorize lots of names and dates. I can't do that.

I really liked all the students in my class. Our class gained a special reputation for being naughty. Some of the best moments at school occurred during the breaks. We were very playful. We love filling balloons with water and throwing them at one another.

My favorite person on the staff at school was a secretary. We always asked her for help when we had problems. But I had problems with most of the school administrators and teachers. They just didn't understand young people of our age. They treat us as if we were their age.

All my friends come from my class at school. I have one best female friend whom I've known for six years. I visit my girlfriend at her home, and I often sleep there. We go for walks on the shore and eat together at restaurants. I also like being friends with boys, and I have a male friend. When I need to talk about problems, I prefer talking with my male friend. There's no jealousy among boys.

On my girlfriend's birthday, we planned to spend the evening together and sleep in our old house. We decided to go to a nightclub. No one knew about this, except for my parents. We didn't tell my girlfriend's parents because we knew her parents disapproved of her going to a bar. But we had a great time, and no one from her family ever found out about it.

After school, I used to play the piano. I studied piano for three years, but I didn't really enjoy the experience. My parents wanted me to continue, but I stopped. I do enjoy dance, however, and I perform in dance concerts. Dancing is my favorite hobby.

I'm not that religious. I can't remember the last time I was in church. I believe that life continues after death. Sometimes I feel that after someone dies, God will forgive them their sins. If I do something wrong and if I then forgive myself, I believe God will forgive me.

I speak Arabic, English, and Hebrew. I would love to learn to speak Italian or German, especially if I were living in these countries. When I hear other languages spoken on the street, I wish I understood them all and could talk with the people speaking them.

When I think about politics, my thoughts immediately turn to the prime minister of Israel. He's the head of state, but he's a person without integrity. I don't like Israeli political leaders in general. They make me, a Palestinian, feel like a foreigner in my own land. The country's leaders are just not honest people. They don't treat us justly. It upsets me that we don't get to learn the history of Palestine in our schools.

"If I had to stay at home for even two days in a row, I'd get very bored. What about those Palestinians who can't move from one city to another for weeks, months, years at a time?"

The biggest problem is the Occupation. Children from both sides, Palestinians and Israelis, are being killed. This is the fault of the Israeli government. All countries evolve, and there is no occupation in the world except for the Israeli Occupation of Palestine. Palestinians are deprived of everything. They don't have freedom to move about. In my case, if I had to stay at home for even two days in a row, I'd get very bored. What about those Palestinians who can't move from one city to another for weeks, months, years at a time?

The solution is that Israel must stop the Occupation immediately. The Israelis want all the land, and this is unjust. There will not be peace with such leaders as those currently in power in Israel.

I used to think that I'd like to leave the country. But I've changed my mind. I realize that I'm an educated person who has a family here, and I want to stay here, close to all my friends. Everyone would like to be rich, but this is not my primary goal in life. If I were to suddenly become wealthy, I'd continue my studies and help my sisters complete their studies as well.

CHAPTER 25

SHIR

"As a counselor I'd have a chance to influence others to be better people. I'd especially like to have some impact on the violence I see all around me."

My name is Shir Klibanski. I'm fourteen years old, going into ninth grade in Itzhak Rabin Junior High School in Rishon LeZion, a city not far from Tel Aviv. I have three brothers, two of them from my father's previous marriage. We fight about everything. We argue about who gets to watch the television in the living room. That's silly, because everyone has a television in their own room. One of my brothers loves to work with computers, but I really don't understand much about them. When I try to work with computers, I mainly wind up destroying them. My father has to come and repair the damage I've done.

This year I applied to join a special group for counselors. I got involved with this project after I got a letter in the mail saying that if we're chosen, we'll get to learn how to improve our self-image, how to counsel others, and how to do some other interesting things. We had to take a test to be accepted into the group. They were trying to see how cooperative we were.

After school my daily routine consists of watching television and spending time at the mall. But on Fridays my friends and I do special things. Rishon LeZion is a great place to live. We really don't lack anything we need. We go bowling and then we go see a movie. Some of my girlfriends have been my friends from early childhood. Others are from elementary school and junior high. Almost all my friends live nearby. Some of them are OK. Maybe I feel that way because I sometimes think I'm better than most other people.

I have some negative thoughts about Israel. I really dislike the arrogance of Israelis. But I also think that people here are warmer and closer to each other than they are in many other countries. As a counselor I'd have a chance to influence others to be better people. I'd especially like to have some impact on the violence I see all around me. But that won't be easy. We're mainly a violent society. The fact that as a counselor I could explain that to small children doesn't mean that these children would necessarily change their ways. That kind of education usually starts from the way children are raised at home.

When I get to high school, I'd like to enter the communications track. Everything that's connected to communications interests me, especially photography. When I grow up, I want to be a writer. Once I thought about being a lawyer. Even now I'm not completely eliminating this as an option for me. When I consider my future, I think I'd also like to volunteer somewhere because it seems important to me to help others. I'd like to volunteer for a project having to do with needy children.

I'm interested in political matters, but only if they're connected to me. If something bad happens in the country, I usually won't go to a protest or anything like that. But if it's really related to me and if it doesn't seem right, then I'll try to work for change. For example,

"I think it would be interesting to meet Palestinian children who are the same age as I am. It'd be interesting to hear what they think."

recently I participated in a protest rally in Rabin Square in Tel Aviv. It was about supporting the disengagement from Gaza. That idea seems like a good one to me, because the Palestinians found this place. But I'm sure that a Jew living in the Gaza Strip won't agree with me. In his mind, it's his home. But I think that nothing is worth soldiers being killed over it.

Peace to me means living without fearing death, without having people close by who want to kill you. The way the situation is now, I feel fear. And I don't think it will be possible to live without fear in the near future. People are not really making an effort to evacuate the settlers. At most they'll be evacuated and then return, so what will happen then? People chose Sharon to be prime minister because they thought he would never agree to have the kind of peace that means giving up land. Most people just prefer to protect their own homes, to defend the place where they live. They would be ready to give up their lives just so that they could keep their homes. When people don't want peace, there won't be any.

I don't think the Palestinians want peace either. But I think that if they had no other choice, then they would agree to have peace. I think it would be interesting to meet Palestinian children who are the same age as I am. It'd be interesting to hear what they think. I've never tried to meet a Palestinian on my own, so I really don't know how successful the meeting would be. I study Arabic in school. It's important for me to learn Arabic so that I can communicate with Palestinians.

When I think about the future, I imagine the best world possible. I dream about a world where there would be harmony. I'd be able to go to the mall or to a coffee shop without fear. I would like all fear to disappear. And I'd like to live this way in Israel, because after all it's my country.

CHAPTER 26

SANDY

"We try to listen carefully to each other in our family, because all problems can be resolved through dialogue."

My name is Sandy Hanna. I'm seventeen years old and live in Ramallah. I go to school at the Rahbat Mar Yusif Tawjih School. My mother passed away. My brother, two sisters, and I live with my father. Juliana is nine years old and is in the fourth grade, and Yara is entering the tenth grade. My brother's name is Gearge.

I like family occasions and holiday celebrations. At those times the atmosphere in the family is especially wonderful. It's good to live with people who care about you. I can turn to my family for help whenever I need to. I have wonderful memories of my mother. She was and still is my ideal person. My mother could do anything. She had a sixth sense about things. My father and I are like the closest of friends. When there's a misunderstanding between us, I get anxious. My sisters and I often argue about what we're going to watch on TV. And I sometimes argue with Yara about who's going to wear certain clothes.

We respect one another in our family. We try to listen carefully to each other, because all problems can be resolved through good dialogue. What's also needed is a clear understanding of what's permitted and what's not permitted in the household. Everyone needs to agree to the rules of the household. For example, after a certain hour it's understood that everyone must complete their studies and turn off the lights. And there are clear rules about when we're allowed to go out of the house and what time we're supposed to return.

I like everyone at school—my girlfriends, the teachers, and administrators. I feel they understand me and are always ready to help me. But this doesn't mean that I'm equally close to all my teachers. My English and math teachers are the ones I'm closest to. But there's one thing that's not so great about school: I have to get up early in order to get there! It's just so hard to get out of bed so early in the morning.

To me, friendship has no age limits, no boundaries. It's a relationship that involves sacrifice and mutual understanding. You should be able to express yourself openly with your friends. I have two close friends. I think of them as sisters. I trust them. They're clever, and they keep secrets. They cry with me and laugh with me. I remember when it snowed two years ago. We went out to play in the empty streets. The snow was beautiful.

I don't only have female friends. I have some male friends. There is no problem as long as there are clear boundaries to these relationships. I like my friends very much. They feel comfortable with me. I would never reveal a secret that a friend had told me. And I'd make sacrifices for my friends. Jesus sacrificed himself for others. I have no problem making sacrifices.

I personally don't like lying, but lying is something basic in life. It's a way to cover up faults in a way that's clever. The last time I lied, I felt

"I write about homeless children in Jenin and about my homeland. I've written about how a child is seen crying on television and about how people turn off their television sets because they can't bear to see this."

compelled to do so in order not to anger a friend whom we were excluding from an outing. My other friends and I went to the seashore, but we told her we weren't going.

After school I go to Al-Sariyah club and study the *dabka*. There are many people who are simply not interested in learning the *dabka*, but they go to the club because there are problems in the city and because the Israeli checkpoints limit our ability to go to other places. I also like swimming; I tried to find a swim club to practice my swimming. I wanted to sign up to participate in competitions, but, alas, I couldn't find any. I was dreaming when I thought I'd like to try out for the Olympics. I didn't have a chance. Anyone who tries out for the Olympics has to work hard from the time she's very young. The only chance for me to try out for the Olympics would be for me to travel to Jerusalem, but my identity card doesn't permit me to go in and out of Jerusalem. We Palestinians are living under the Israeli Occupation. We can't travel from one place to another without permission, because the stronger party is the ruler, and that's Israel. Israel prohibits us from entering Jerusalem unless we have permission, so I can't practice my swimming.

I'm a Christian. If I want to follow the teachings of Jesus Christ, I should be forgiving even of Jews in Israel. If I do something bad, I'm sure God will forgive me. God lives in the soul of every one of us. I'm not sure where a person goes when he dies, but I try to be good as I can be, so that I will go to heaven.

I wish I lived in Jerusalem so that I could go and pray in the Church of the Holy Sepulchre. But I'm not as religious as my mother was. Christians and Muslims love each other, and we don't have any problems. We regard ourselves as Palestinians first, before being either Muslims or Christians.

I think about the leader of my country and about the leader of Israel. I respect the president of the Palestinian people. I pray for him, because he is jailed in his headquarters Al-Muqata and can't get out. It's hard to be in your country and not move about freely. The prime minister of Israel is a person who doesn't know how to think. I don't know how his conscience permits him to sleep, since he's responsible for the killing of innocent children.

I just don't see how the current conflict will be resolved. Talking will not help, but I hope there will be a peace agreement. I don't have any problem with Israelis. But the Israelis must let us live, because we're very tired.

An important interest of mine is writing. I write about myself, about my family, and about my homeland. I've written about homeless children in Jenin, about how a child is seen crying on television and about how people turn off their television sets because they can't bear to see this. I also write poetry. Here's one of my favorite lines of poetry: "Damned are those who see tears on an innocent child's face, the child whose mother is killed, the child who will be lost."

I speak Arabic, English, and French. I'm also studying Italian, and I'd like to continue studying in Italy someday. I don't use the Hebrew language. When I come to the checkpoints, I speak English with the Israeli soldiers. I would only have to use Hebrew at the checkpoints, so why do I have to learn this language?

If I were to win a million dollars, I'd build a swimming pool. I'd also create a project for children who like reading and writing, because we have many talented children in Palestine who don't have anyone to help them.

CHAPTER 27

SHIRLI

"It's a major problem that Palestinians and Israelis
don't visit one another in a normal way."

I'm Shirli, and I'm eighteen years old. I live in Kfar Saba with my parents and my brother, who's thirteen. Everything is basically OK in the family. We all enjoy going to the seashore and having fun together. I like the holidays, but how good they are depends upon whom we invite from our very large family. We all mean well in our relationships with one another.

There are some very good moments with the family, and there are some moments when we're very sad. We had a difficult time when my grandfather died. Then a second grandfather died two weeks later. I overcame this hard time by telling myself that we have to go on, we have to live.

I think my parents are overprotective. This bothers me. When I have children, I'll care for them in a way that they won't feel as restricted as I've felt in my home. When I get married, I think I'll choose to marry a Jew. It's important for me and for my parents. But if I were to meet a kind and wealthy Christian, I don't know if I would prefer him to a Jewish man who is less wealthy and less kind. However, being married and having children do not occupy my thoughts right now.

Studying appeals to me. I attend the Rabin School in Kfar Saba. It's a very new school. Teachers in my school are very close to their students. I especially like physics and math. After the army, I'll choose between studying engineering and studying special education, which would prepare me for working with children with learning disabilities. And I've always wanted to learn more about astronomy. Perhaps I'll decide to enter that field in the future.

I don't know if I'll stay in Kfar Saba in the future. But for now I love Kfar Saba. It's familiar to me, and I don't know where else I would live. It's funny that all the young people leave Kfar Saba and go to Tel Aviv. In Tel Aviv there are many young people, but few families. The city is not well balanced in this way.

I have friends, but I haven't had any serious troubles in my life that have made me seek help from them. To me, a friend is someone who cares about you, someone you have fun with. A friend helps you when you're in a trouble. When I get together with my friends, we often go to see a movie. I love watching films. I go to the movies whenever I can. There was a time when I used to watch as many as four films a day.

I like all Israeli music. I'm also attracted to Um Kalthum. I want to develop my voice. I started to study voice with my neighbor, who's a voice teacher. But she forced me to learn a song in Italian. I didn't like doing this, so I ended my lessons with her. Also, I'm afraid to stand on the stage and sing. Singing is just a hobby. One can't make a living that way.

I'm an Israeli citizen because I was born in Israel. An Arab who is born in East Jerusalem cannot obtain Israeli citizenship. This bothers me, but I've no easy solution to offer. It's a problematic situation. People just don't connect with one another. There are citizens who were born here in earlier years. Then people came from all over the world and decided to settle here. There is a big problem here concerning the issue of citizenship. I'm not totally sure of my right to live here.

There was a project in my city that involved visiting Palestinians, but my mother didn't allow me to participate in these visits. She thought that there would be some risk in my getting involved with the project. I think that this was a matter of stereotyping. It's a major problem that Palestinians and Israelis don't visit one another in a normal way. When I enter the army, I'm going to study Arabic for a month and a half. There are many people of my age who know every-thing about the conflict, but I'm not one of them. I listen to the news, but it brings me to the point of despair instead of moving me to take some action or make up my mind about an issue. I myself don't have any ambition to be involved in politics.

To bring peace, the Palestinian Authority should return money they've stolen from the people. As for Ariel Sharon, he's a leader with no vision. I don't trust him. If he were honest, I'd have voted for him. The most important thing that a leader has to have is personal integrity. One leader whom I consider to have excelled in his position was Men-achem Begin. He used to travel around the country by bus. Also Churchill was a superb head of state. These two were intelligent leaders, politicians who were available to ordinary people.

In Iraq those who are making war are acting according to an illusion. People are being killed. Ordinary people are dying. The leaders play with the world as if it were a toy. The world is full of conflicts. I think what ordinary people do or fail to do is really important. I think peace starts from the people. Conflicts are not really between states, because states and countries are made up of people. The most important thing is for people to begin to understand one another.

I believe in God, but I don't believe in the justice of the way God acts. My path to God is to be OK within myself. People want someone to look after them, they don't want to feel alone. For this reason, I believe the idea of God was first conceived. I feel close to God when I see other people, especially when I see the little things that people do. I don't have much knowledge about other religions. I know more about Christianity than about Islam. Islam is a religion that started from Muhammad, who is considered the last prophet. I've heard about the Muslim feast days, but I don't know a lot about them.

I'd like to visit many places in the world, such as Europe, India, and South America. I lived in California, in the United States, for two years. I went there because my father was sent to California in connection with his duties at work. People in the United States think a lot about peace. Here, in Israel, people are crushed by day-to-day reality. I don't see my future clearly, but I know I want to feel whole within myself.

CHAPTER 28
SARI

"I want to
help everyone
who's
oppressed.
We all need a
better life."

My name is Sari. I'm fifteen years old and live in Tira. I have an older sister and two younger brothers. Sometimes my dad treats me as a friend, sometimes as a son. There are very few arguments among members of our family. I do remember one argument, but it wasn't all that serious. About a year ago my mother wanted to go for a walk with my father. Wanting to tease my mom, my father said, "I'm busy, you go for a walk." My mother was angry, but my father apologized and told her he was only joking.

I always feel happy when I'm with my family, but that doesn't mean we don't experience difficult times, like times when someone is sick or someone dies. My neighbor's son—only ten years old—died in an accident when a large stone fell on him. We were saddened by this loss.

No matter how good relationships are between teachers and students, there's often some tension felt. I've had some experiences that are stressful. At the end of a class, I like to stand near the door. I just don't like sitting in my chair all the time. One teacher disapproved of my standing up. I told him I was not harming anyone and that I would prefer not to do anything different from what I was doing. If I were the principal of the school, I would certainly urge the teachers to be more flexible in the way they treat students. I would order them to give students more freedom.

After school I enjoy playing my guitar. I take guitar lessons on a regular basis. I like music in general, but I especially enjoy music from Latin America. Spanish-speaking countries are full of life. Because they're so lively, these countries will no doubt thrive in others areas of life as well. My favorite singer is Shakira, a Colombian singer whose father is Lebanese. Playing the guitar while I'm listening to Shakira's music is a wonderful experience! If I had the opportunity, I'd love to become a famous musician someday. But to achieve this, I'd have to continue my guitar studies and take them more and more seriously. If I can't achieve this goal for some reason, I'll at least make certain that I teach my children the music I love.

One day I'll meet Shakira at one of her concerts, and I'll tell her

"My favorite singer is Shakira. . . . One day I'll meet Shakira, and I'll tell her about myself."

about myself. I may attract her interest. If she would agree to a face-to-face interview, I'll explain to her how much I like her songs and how well I play guitar. Shakira's sweet songs connect me to God. They nourish my soul. The meaning of the words of her songs is communicated beautifully through the music.

I also like writing my own songs. I wrote a song as a tribute to a person who is strong, someone whose life is as beautiful as a rose. When I wrote this song of tribute, I imagined dedicating it to all oppressed peoples, everyone who has had to make sacrifices by having to go to war. This includes both Palestinians and also other oppressed peoples with whom I'm not so familiar. I want to help everyone who's oppressed. We all need a better life.

We all need friends. Friendship is something that unites people as if they were brothers. Friends are linked by feelings of love, respect, and trust. I don't have one best friend. I've always been uncomfortable deciding which friend is number one in my life. I belong to a wonderful group of four friends. We're all close to one another. These special friends make a real effort to celebrate my birthday every year with a wonderful party. Last year, we had a huge gathering, including lots of members of my family. My friends are all boys. In our society it's just not customary for boys and girls to hang out together on the street.

I hope that the political situation in Israel will improve. The prime minister of Israel is a smart man, but I don't admire his kind of intelligence. The prime minister is the reason there's a second Intifada. He's not even good for Israelis. For example, he ordered the soldiers to occupy Palestinian lands and kill innocent people. And Palestinian martyrs came, exploded themselves, and killed Israelis. So—indirectly—Sharon is killing his own people! If I were in his place, I'd make peace with Palestinians. I'd make certain that there would be a Palestinian state. I would tell the Palestinian people not to end their struggle until peace is achieved.

If I were to become wealthy, I'd donate money to poor Palestinians, and I'd give some to my family and friends. I'd also give some of my money to Shakira's organization, which is dedicated to peacemaking.

CHAPTER 29
TAL

"I'd like to be an actress someday. I want everyone to know who Tal is."

I'm Tal. I'm twelve years old, and I live in Mevasseret Tzion, near Jerusalem. I live with my mother, father, and a brother and sister who are both younger than I am.

The school I'll be going to next year is a boarding school called Nachlat Yehuda. I'll be entering seventh grade this fall. It's a new school for me. I'm transferring to Nachlat Yehuda because I heard some not so nice things about the junior high in my own city. That school wasn't the one my mom thought it would be good for me to attend. I'll be living, as well as studying, in my new school.

I had a wonderful time visiting my new school. Inside, there are some large rooms, big enough to hold all two hundred fifty students. I had a good feeling about what it would be like to be a student there. Right now when I think about leaving home, I don't have any negative feelings. But when the time comes in the fall, I may well feel homesick. I know I'll miss my little sister most of all. She's always by my side. We've never been apart. Because we're so tight, it'll be especially hard for me to leave her.

My new school also has a chicken coop and a cow shed. I love all animals, but I'm especially attached to dolphins, horses, and dogs. Dolphins because they're cute, horses because of their strength and speed, and dogs because I once had one. I could tell her secrets that she would never reveal to anyone.

I didn't like most of my studies in my old school—except for my Torah studies. The other subjects bore me—especially math. All those numbers! I like Torah because I like reading stories. Not just any stories, like the ones we read in Hebrew literature classes, but biblical stories, which I find touching. One other subject—drama—also attracted me. My best grades were in drama. There, you didn't have to write things down in your notebook, and you didn't have to memorize material.

I like acting, both in school and even at home. At school, I participated in the drama club. We had a big end-of-year party, and I took part in a play we put on. At home I practice my acting skills by attempting to trick mother into letting me stay home from school. It's fun. I pretend

"It's not so much the responsibility of leaders
to achieve peace. It's the responsibility of people."

I'm sick. But when she discovers that it's all just an act, she gets angry and orders me to head for school immediately.

I'd like to be an actress someday. I'll first want to be successful in Israel, then on to Hollywood. What I especially like about acting is the possibility of achieving fame and becoming rich. I want everyone to know who Tal is. I know there are other ways of becoming famous and wealthy. But when you're a famous actor or a singer, it's worth all the effort. If you're a doctor, or something like that, it's also possible that you'll get recognition from some people, but after a short while, you're forgotten. That's not so when you're a famous actor.

After school I come home and turn on the TV. Then I take my brother to the playground. I help Mother hang laundry and take out the garbage—things like that. By then it's evening, and Mom and I will sit down to watch our favorite TV programs. My sister goes to sleep early, and then I go to bed. We share the same room. When our room becomes messy, I push things into a corner, hoping Mom won't see all the clutter.

I also spend time after school babysitting young twin girls. I got the job because their mother came to the park once and watched me taking care of my little brother. She understood that I knew how to care for children, and she asked me if I could babysit for her girls. I enjoy earning my own money. I'm trying to save a lot of it, and Mother helps me by checking daily to see if I've spent it or if I'm really saving what I earn. If I were to receive a gift of money, however, I'd immediately go and buy clothes with it—pants, sleeveless shirts, and jeans. I'd choose the kind of clothing that I like, not the kind my mother would prefer me to wear. I'd love to be rich. If I were to win the lottery, I'd spend it all. I wouldn't need to share with others in need, because there are other rich people who could do that.

One time I wanted to buy a pair of pants, but I didn't have enough money to buy the pair I wanted. So I asked my mom to buy the pants for me. She refused, saying that they were too short. I screamed at her and told her she was a bad mother and that I would not talk with her for the rest of my life. But not-talking-to-my-mom lasted only an hour.

Once, on a school trip, we slept away from home, in a youth hostel.

It was a wonderful experience, because when you're at the hostel, your mother doesn't pester you to go to sleep at a certain time. You can be with your girlfriends and share secrets. The only problem was that some of the girls went to sleep too early!

I have a very good friend, someone who's always on my side. No matter what happens, she'll always be my friend, even if we argue sometimes. I remember one argument. My friend broke my little sister's mirror, and I got really angry at her. If it had been my own mirror, I'm not sure I would have reacted that way. Although I've not completely forgotten about this incident, I'm no longer angry about it. It was about a mirror—a pretty stupid thing to have an argument about.

My neighborhood in Mevasseret is quite diverse. There are many communities living together—religious and secular. There's a synagogue across the street from my house. My father attends services there. He doesn't care whether or not I play with religious kids. But the neighborhood also has some kids whom I don't like to hang out with. Some of the girls wear miniskirts, and they form cliques. But I do enjoy some activities with the neighborhood kids. There's a playground where everyone goes to play soccer and handball. Although I enjoy playing handball, I've never considered becoming a professional athlete. I easily get hurt playing sports. I've broken both my hands and my nose. Occasionally I'll watch a soccer game with my dad on TV, but I really don't understand what's going on—only that twenty-two men are running after a ball.

I don't feel connected to any religion, but I know I'm Jewish. My father prays, and mother does not allow me to wear a miniskirt. On Friday night we say kiddush, and on Saturday we don't use the stove. I like the kiddush, because the wine is tasty, but I won't want to have this ritual in my own home. It delays dinner. And I don't particularly believe in God. It depends on the situation. If I'm stuck in an elevator, I would ask God to save me. But I'm not sure that we were created by God. It's possible that we came from a monkey. But then the question is who created the monkey. It's a complicated issue. I don't know a lot about other religions. I believe that when people die, they go to the Garden of Eden.

That's a place where animals can talk and a place where people are always young.

As for the political situation, I try to avoid listening to or watching the news. There was only one political leader I had faith in: Rabin. His path was one of peace and love. It seems to me that he was responsible for lots of peace agreements. I liked him because he paid attention to people. He knew that people were suffering, and he tried to improve their situation. I think that even now we can learn to live together in peace with the Palestinians. But Sharon would have to no longer be our prime minister. Something can be done. It's possible to talk to Palestinians and to get to know their feelings. It would be good to know their weaknesses, too. For example, my weakness is my strong attachment to my dog. I felt helpless when my dog died. It's possible that a Palestinian had a dog who died or who is dying. It's possible that he'll realize that he doesn't want people to die like his dog did. Emotions work.

Also, it's not so much the responsibility of leaders to achieve peace. It's the responsibility of people. We should not fight with one other. We should work together, like members of a team.

CHAPTER 30
SHARIHAN

"My parents always support me in everything I do, because they know that if something is wrong, I simply won't do it."

My name is Sharihan. I was born in 1987 in Abu-Ghosh, a small village next to Jerusalem. I'm related to all my neighbors. This is something special. Not many people have their relatives living right near them.

I have two sisters and two brothers, all of whom are younger than I am. I have a great time with my brothers. We make a game out of everything we do. If we have an argument, the bad feelings are quickly forgotten. By the next day it's as if nothing had every happened.

My parents have given me a lot of freedom to choose my own path in life. Whatever restrictions there are in my life are ones I've imposed on myself. My parents always support me in everything I do, because they know that if something is wrong, I simply won't do it. There was a time when I was uncertain whether or not to cover my hair according to Muslim tradition. My parents encouraged me to do it, but they didn't force me.

I used to go swimming in Maaleh Hahamisha. That was when I was young. But at age thirteen I stopped going swimming. God knows better than I what's right and what's wrong. Even though I don't always understand why things are the way they are, I just have faith in Allah.

I pray five times a day, I fast, and I'll go to Haj when I grow up. A lot of people think that Islam is a complicated religion, but I don't think that's so. It's comprehensive, but it's also a very simple religion. We have to think about what Allah has given us. Even if we don't have a lot of material possessions, the smallest things should still be appreciated by us. Islam has positive effects on my personality. It helps me to grow spiritually.

I attend American high school in Jerusalem. I've just completed the eleventh grade. Whether a class is good or not depends a great deal on how good the teacher is. My history teacher, for example, is an excellent teacher. He's very knowledgeable about everything—not only about history, but also about science, religion, and math. The subject I like most in school is algebra. I don't know why I like it. I just do. I'm a math person.

At school, everybody knows each other. This makes day-to-day life at school a lot easier. I help my classmates when they have trouble understanding the teacher. I have two best friends, one of whom I've known since nursery school. We've grown up together. She's very shy, but kind. She's always smiling and laughing. I like her personality.

This summer I participated in a camp in Maine in the United States. "Seeds of Peace" is a very exceptional camp. Every person should have the chance to be a "seed of peace." This camp is international. People from all over the world come to America to be a part of

"People can always disagree with each other but still be friends."

this camp. When I was there, there were delegations from Palestine, Israel, India, Pakistan, Afghanistan, Jordan, Egypt, Morocco, and the United States. What I learned from attending this camp is that people can always disagree with each other but still be friends and live peacefully together. You can be very wrong about what "the other side" is like, and they could be wrong about what you're like. You can be surprised at what they think about you. In this camp you have the chance to talk freely and say whatever you want. People like you for your personality and don't value you on the basis of where you come from.

If I could choose where to live, I'd choose to live in Dubai. Dubai has incorporated many positive aspects of American life. I appreciate the fact that Dubai, as a Muslim and Arab country, is tolerant of Western lifestyles. And since English is one of the languages spoken in Dubai, I'd feel especially comfortable living there. I like speaking English as much as Arabic.

If I were to become rich, I'd help my family be comfortable, because if I spend my money on peacemaking in the world and my family does not have what it needs, I'd feel guilty. My father and mother have spent all their money on me—especially on my education. I would never be able to pay them back, but I still think it's my responsibility to make them as comfortable as possible. After that was accomplished, I would look for ways to make peace.

I have a lot of admiration for Gandhi. Gandhi brought peace and liberty to his country, and he did it without using violence. I'd like my county to be free and to be without violence. I'd like to make a difference in the world. I'd also like to walk on the moon someday.

CHAPTER 31

URI

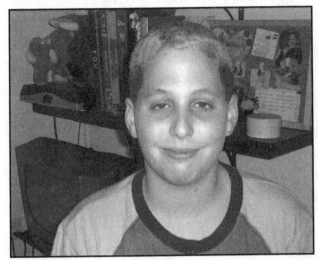

"I sometimes act in an immature way. My grandma always asks me, 'What will happen when you go into the army?' I tell her that in my soul I'll always be a child."

My name is Uri Eisenberg, and I live in Rishon LeZion. There are five people in my family, and one dog. I'm the youngest. My twin sister was born two minutes ahead of me. We're both fourteen and a half. My big sister is twenty-four.

My relationship with my father is excellent. We go to the movies a lot, and he also takes me bowling every week. That's really nice. Not every parent can do this. He also helps me prepare for tests, even though he's not home a lot. Every time I bring friends home, he socializes with them, telling jokes. I love my dad. He's a very caring person.

My mom and I don't have as good a relationship as the one I have with my dad. She worries too much about me. Sometimes she gets angry with me, whether or not I'm at fault for what happened. We fight a lot, although I think there'll be fewer fights in the future. I'm just not that mature yet. I'd like to talk with my mother so that I can understand her better. I'd like to tell her what's happening with me. But often our fights make this impossible. When we're not fighting, I do try to involve her in my life, and sometimes she'll take me out for something to eat or drink. At those times, I do confide in her. But there are still things that I don't tell my mother. I'm jealous of other kids who go on lots of outings with *both* their parents.

My older sister, Tal, and I are not that close. She doesn't realize how much I respect her. I feel that when she needs a favor, she calls me. I've not been to her apartment since she moved out of our home. She's never invited me. I don't feel we have much of a relationship at this point in time. Maybe when I grow up things will improve.

Tamar is my twin sister. I love her. We fight, but I'm to blame for most of these quarrels. We're like cat and mouse, chasing each other and sometimes hitting each other. However, she knows it's all in fun and that I love her. I like Tamar's personality. She knows just how to help me when I need it.

It's said that having a twin brother or sister is a good thing. In my opinion it's not all that good. My sister and I sometimes make fun of each other, and occasionally we wind up not talking to each other for a whole week. It's not great that we're in the same grade level in school. Our friends call us "test-tube twins." They enjoy the fact that we really are test-tube babies, but I certainly don't like being called that.

When I'm angry or when I'm fighting with my sister, I've begun to learn to let go of my anger by sitting down and drawing pictures. I love drawing. It helps me forget my problems.

When I act in an immature way or fight with my sister, my grandma always says to me, "You're almost fifteen years old. Will you continue to act this way? What will happen when you go into the army?" I tell her that in my soul I'll always be a child. But I know I really have to mature. I also know that I haven't matured yet. I still don't have any hair on my chest.

My grandma is very important to me. We go to her home for lunch every Wednesday. She moved from Ramat Gan to Rishon just to be near us. My grandma spends all day cooking. When we arrive on Wednesdays, we just can't wait for the food to be ready. It's the best food, the tastiest—better than Mom's or Dad's food. I feel at home in her house.

At home we eat separately. It's not good that we don't eat together. Sharing meals can improve family relationships. Also it's fun to eat together. It's great if you can talk about all that's happened to you during the past week. We eat lunch together only on the Sabbath. Being together on the Sabbath is important, because it also allows us to follow our tradition. We invite Grandma or other people for Sabbath meals. I love having guests in my house.

I like elderly people. I don't know why, but I always seem to get close to them. I have an older neighbor in the building, and I speak with her when I have time before I leave for school. I also volunteer in a community center. Truthfully, I don't have much time because of all the homework they give us, but I really try to go to the center every Thursday. I collect vegetables and other goods for the old people. I feel

"I feel sad when violence breaks out, because I think we're all human beings. ... It's an uneasy feeling when you know that we hurt them and that they hurt us in return."

like I'm helping when I give them things they wouldn't ordinarily have. You feel like you're contributing.

I dream of living someday in a big house with a lot of property and a dog running in the yard. We've already had two dogs. Three years ago we were out with our parents. A dog off the leash bit our first dog. She died. Then my older sister cried and begged our parents to get another dog. I think Dad was moved by Tal's tears. They went out together and came home with the dog we have now, a pure-bred poodle called Tisho.

I attend Mordei Hagetaot Junior High School. I'm generally accepted by my classmates, though I'm not in the "in" group in my grade level. Soon I'll be ready for high school. I don't feel like going to the school near my house, because it doesn't have good teachers. If a friend decides to join me, I'd love to go to an academic high school and study math. I'm really good in math. I've even thought about going into that field when I grow up. However, the high school that offers math is far away. If it doesn't work out for me to attend that school, I could study photography at a school closer to Rishon.

I like languages. I'd like to speak many languages and I'm trying to learn as many as possible, so that when I go to different countries I'll be able to speak the native tongue. I had a choice between Arabic and French. I chose French, because I have uncles and cousins in Belgium. When I visit during vacations, it will be helpful if I can speak French with them. My father is French, and he always helps me. It's a lot of fun doing homework with him. I feel that when I visit my uncles during vacation periods, we'll get close to one another because we'll be speaking a common language.

I know for sure what I'll be when I grow up. I like designing things—whole houses, rooms, and furniture. If you walk into my room, you'll see how my ideas about design have become real. I took some calendars from a book about cars and hung them on the wall. This gives the room a certain aesthetic feel. I placed a chair in my room, put paint on my hand, and imprinted the chair with the paint. The chair looks great. Many of my friends have complimented me on the way it looks. It's important to know that you'll be working in a profession you really like. Law, which is my father's profession, doesn't interest me at all. I was always told it doesn't matter what you work at, as long as you feel good about what you've chosen. Design and architecture have always appealed to me. I think I'll go for it.

With regard to the political situation, I think we need to make peace. I don't have anything against Palestinians. They're a people like us. It's not the fault of the entire Palestinian people that there are some who throw stones or hurt soldiers. I don't think they're really different from us. Certainly their children are educated in ways that are similar to the ways we're educated. I feel sad when violence breaks out because I think we're all human beings. We need to stop fighting. It's an uneasy feeling when you know that we hurt them and that they hurt us in return. Sometimes on TV I hear people cursing Palestinians. I think that's not right.

My view on the conflict is different from my friends' views. My friends tend to say the exact opposite. They say that it's the Palestinians who cause all the hatred and war. I think this is absolutely false. Those that cause wars have to be stopped, but others are people just like us, just as nice as we are.

I feel the same way about people coming from different religious traditions. I have no problem with other religions. We all believe in the same God. There are really no differences between Christians, Muslims, and Jews.

CHAPTER 32
SIREEN

"I like horses and birds because they symbolize the freedom that Palestinians don't have."

My name is Sireen. I'm seventeen years old and live in Jerusalem with my mom and dad. I have two sisters and one brother, all of them younger than I am. My sisters and I try to be more like friends than sisters. They always seek my opinion about stuff. But when I tell them something they don't like, they start arguing with me. I tell them it's up to them whether they want to listen to me or not. Everyone is entitled to their own thinking.

I have lots of disagreements with my parents. We have different points of view because they're adults and I'm a teenager. I want to do everything in my own way. For example, when my family plans a visit to my grandparents' house, my parents want me to join them. But I'd rather go to my friend's house. My parents don't accept this. I prefer being with my friends because we're the same age, we think the same, and we have fun together. Sometimes I listen to my parents and go with them, and sometimes I don't.

My parents and I also disagree about my choice of where to go to college. I want to go to a college far away from home—in America or in Lebanon—but they want me to go college in Palestine. They think I'm still a child, that I'll have lots of problems if I leave Palestine. They say that after four years I'll be mature and then I can go abroad to live. I have to obey my parents, because I believe they want the best for me. I'm their daughter. I've talked with many people about this, and they've encouraged me to stay close to my family.

My parents have some definite rules that I have to follow at home. I am not to go out without permission, and I'm not to stay out late on school days. These rules I accept. Rules teach us that our freedom stops where others' freedom starts. When I want to watch a TV program and my brother wants to watch cartoons, I wind up watching my program for an hour, and he watches his cartoons for an hour. Without rules we would fight, because my brother would want to watch cartoons all the time. If I become a parent, I'll enforce rules like these. I'll never allow my children to cross a certain line. I'll not allow them to do what I do to my parents. When I go to my friend's house, my Mom tells me to call her to let her know that I'm OK. But I often forget, and she keeps waiting for my call. I won't let my children forget; I'll call them.

I'll allow them to go and sleep at a friend's house, but I'll try to convince them that it's better to sleep at home because of security concerns. We live under Occupation and it's hard to travel and sleep at my friend's house. My parents won't allow me to sleep at her house because they worry about me. My friends live in Ramallah. There are checkpoints on the way, and it's difficult to know what's going to happen. Anybody at any time can be taken out of their house or shot in Ramallah. My parents want to protect us. They wouldn't know what's happening with me while I'm in Ramallah. That's why I'm not allowed to sleep there. If I were a parent in this situation I would do the same, but I hope that by the time I become a parent, the situation will improve and I'll be able to allow my children to visit Ramallah.

I live in Ras-El-Amud neighborhood in Jerusalem. My neighbors are my relatives, so I just drop in to visit them. The houses have no numbers on them, things that modern cities such as Tel Aviv would have. We have difficulties letting people know where our house is. I'd prefer living in another place—like California. It would be more comfortable. Ras-El-Amud has had a checkpoint near it for the last nine years. When you want to visit another place, you have to think about it a thousand times, because in order to leave the neighborhood, you have to wait an hour and a half just to go through the checkpoint. It's difficult doing this, especially on school days. I had to get up an hour earlier during the school year. Now that the checkpoint has been removed, it takes only fifteen minutes to get to school. That's better. I have an extra seventy-five minutes to sleep. I love to sleep.

The checkpoint used to get on my nerves. It was not necessary to have it. Why put it there? It's just to make us uncomfortable, to make us crazy and nervous. We didn't go out very much because of the checkpoint. The soldiers at the checkpoint were young, just eighteen years old.

I don't like someone coming to my neighborhood and interfering in my life. Someone who is a teenager comes and asks you for your identity card, asks you where you want to go and why you want to go there.

Such questions! Sometimes I answer, and sometimes I just ask them why they're asking all these questions. I tell them it's none of their business; I tell them to get out of my way.

We have a new settlement near our neighborhood. It's less than a year old. It's because of the settlers living there that the checkpoint was removed. These settlers don't interfere much with our lives because they're few in numbers. But God knows what will happen in the future. The Israelis took all of West Jerusalem. Now they want to take East Jerusalem. They're greedy.

Now they're building more new houses and settlements in East Jerusalem because they want to get out of the Gaza Strip and come here. All the Israelis who leave Gaza would come to live here. As long as they don't interfere in our lives and don't destroy our houses, maybe we can live together. But if they do those things, it will be difficult for us.

My school is one of the best schools near Jerusalem. Our headmistress is very strict, but she's good for us. She and the other teachers don't allow us to hang out with the same group of friends all the time, because then other students are made to feel like outsiders. The best thing about school is the opportunity to make new friends.

I hate when our teachers give us lots of homework, leaving me no time to watch TV or to go visiting. I get bored when course material is not interesting. But I like Biology. In this course we talk about interesting things, about human beings. I'm not very quiet in school. I talk a lot in my classes. I ask lots of questions, questions that sometimes are not that relevant. For example, I'll ask my teacher about her vacation. Then she'll forget about the subject we're studying. My friends like these distractions.

I used to love the last day of school because summer vacation was coming, but this year I had to say good-bye to my teachers, my friends, and my school. It wasn't easy for me. I hated the last day. When I remember that day I feel sad; then I immediately call my friends. We didn't have a graduation party. The headmistress didn't want to organize a large gathering because of the political situation. But we had a small party at a hotel. There were photographers there, and music also. We ate dinner with cake for dessert. We had lots of fun.

I hate to lie, but one time I had no choice in the matter. My friend was in a bad situation, and I had to get her out of it, so I lied. A teacher thought my friend was not paying attention in class. She was chatting and laughing with a classmate. The teacher got upset. My friend apologized, but the teacher didn't accept her apology. I went and said to the teacher, "My friend didn't mean not to listen to you. Her classmate was asking her questions about the subject matter, that's why she got distracted." So I helped her get out of this difficult situation. I had to lie; she had asked me for help. I felt bad for lying, but I consider it a white lie.

I have lots of friends. Friendship is very important to me; it comes right after family. My friends are my second family. Families of my best friends consider me a friend of the family too. My friends are honest people and I like their honesty, even if it hurts sometimes. I make friends easily; I'm a social person. My friends are girls. I don't have a boyfriend. My parents forbid me to have a boyfriend because of our tradition. I think having male friends is OK, but it would be silly to have a boyfriend. I have friends who have boyfriends. One day, one of them told me, "We had fun," and then the following day she said, "We broke up." I like having friends who are like brothers. I like sharing secrets with them, expressing feelings, seeking their opinion when I'm in trouble. This type of friendship is better; it lasts longer. If you have a fight with a male friend, you'll get over it in two or three days. But a fight with a boyfriend would break your heart.

I like horses and birds because they symbolize the freedom that Palestinians don't have. I'd like to switch places with birds. Birds have wings and can go wherever they want. I'd like to do the same, I'd like to be free. I love freedom. But I don't feel free inside. Yes, I've traveled to France, Cairo, and Amman, but I always had the feeling I wasn't truly free. My dream is to design a flying car, because at least it would not have to stop at checkpoints. I'd go all different places. One day I'd be in Lebanon, the following day the Caribbean.

I'm a Muslim. We believe in one God. Our prophet taught us what we should and shouldn't do, about what's forbidden and what's not. He taught us that life is only a test for human beings, and if you pass the test, you'll go to heaven. Regardless of our mistakes, if we ask God to forgive us, God will do so, because every person makes mistakes. The important thing is to learn from them. If you don't learn, God will not forgive you. Our religion emphasizes peace, love, and sharing. These are the most important things. We Muslims believe that when one dies, his spirit stays alive. If you do bad things, God will punish you. Fear of punishment prevents you from repeating bad things. I believe in punishment. You must learn from your mistakes.

All of us living here are active politically. We have no choice in the matter. It's possible to resolve the conflict peacefully. I want to have peace with all people who see me as a person. Peace to me means security and living with dignity and respect. I want my children to have these things. If I were in charge, I'd use all my power to build a solid

"Rules teach us that our freedom stops where others' freedom starts."

peace based on dignity and justice. Peace means living in a neighborhood where one doesn't hear shootings. It means people respecting each other for who they are. War means destruction, refugees, people losing their homes, and innocent people losing their lives.

Learning Hebrew is very important because it's the language of our enemies. We have to understand what they say, especially at the checkpoints and at hospitals. Learning Hebrew helps me a lot. Soldiers often are stubborn and won't talk to you except in Hebrew. They start asking questions, and I have to answer them. Also it's important to introduce ourselves to the Jews because I think Jews don't know Palestinians the way they should. They think that we're from the third world, that we don't like learning, that we're not open-minded. They think that we live just to work, just to earn money in order to buy food. But we love learning. We're an educated and open-minded people. Other people take ideas from us. Before the Intifada we had a pharmaceutical industry in Gaza and lots of other countries bought medicine from us. But when the Intifada began, the Israelis destroyed this industry. My uncle used to work there.

If I had to share land, I would do it. It's the only way to solve the problems between Palestinians and Israelis. It won't be a problem sharing land as long as the Israelis respect us and acknowledge our rights. I'd like to live a life full of peace, full of joy. No matter how hard it is to share the land, in the end sharing is the best solution. War, killing innocent people, and destroying the homes of innocent people should never take place. Sometimes Israelis destroy a house where fifteen kids live. They destroy their lives, not only their homes. Peace is the best solution.

In the future I'd like to visit many places: Lebanon, Holland, and the Caribbean. But after having already gone to Egypt, France, and Jordan, I realize that there is no place like home. I'd like to live alone when I'm an adult, but not far from my parents. If I had problems, they would help and support me.

Five years from now I see myself a successful graduate student. Ten years from now I'll be an effective woman with an important role in society. I see myself raising my children, driving them to school, and living in a peaceful environment.

CHAPTER 33

TAMARA

"My ultimate dream is to unite the world,
removing all borders. I'd cancel the names of all countries.
There would be just one flag for one world,
a world of peace."

My name is Tamara Kamal. I'm thirteen years old and have three younger brothers. Our family lives in Abu-Ghosh, a small village near Jerusalem.

I love my village very much. It's small and beautiful. Tourists from all parts of the country and from abroad come to visit. I also love Jerusalem. I go there to shop. I especially realize how much I love Abu-Ghosh when I'm far away from home. The last time I traveled abroad, I went to Turkey and Cyprus. I enjoyed the trip, but I felt lonely and homesick. I missed my grandma a lot. Something in me told me to return home. I'd like to live in Abu-Ghosh all my life, because that's where my family lives.

In my village houses are close to one another. All my relatives— uncles and cousins—live in the same neighborhood. We have eight houses on our block. I feel they're one house. It's quiet, but sometimes it gets noisy, especially when we're out playing. I love my neighborhood. I feel happy in it. We don't have any problems. We know each other very well. When we visit a relative, we just knock on the door and go in. When I visit my friend's mother, I knock on the door, ask, "Are you there?" and then go in. That's it.

My mother helps me a lot with any problems I have. But sometimes we have disagreements. We often argue about clothes. She has her taste, and I have mine. My parents have rules about how long I can stay out with my friends. Even when I visit my grandma's house, which is nearby, my parents tell me that I have to come home by nine o'clock at the latest. If I want to go anyplace, I have to get my parents' permission.

My mother encouraged me to play the piano. Once I played the piano in front of a crowd, but I was shy. The audience was pleased and clapped for me. I played a piece, called in Arabic "*Ah Ya Zehn Ah Ya Zehn Ah Ya Zin El Abideen. Ya Ward Mifatah Bin El Basateen.*" In English this means "Oh beautiful, Oh beautiful, Oh beautiful among mankind, Oh blooming roses among the gardens."

I also like to sing, but only for myself. I feel shy when I have to sing in front of other people—except for my cousin. I sing at home when I'm in a good mood. To learn a new piece, I listen to the whole song first, then I listen to the music only and sing along with it.

Long ago when our very famous singer Um Kalthum sang, she just stood in one place while performing. Today's female singers all move around in their skimpy clothing, something that is not at all fitting for an Arab woman. These performers have abandoned our folklore. Obviously they're imitating Westerners, who move around a lot when they sing. Westerners are not better than we are.

I love school because it prepares me for life. I feel happy when I go to school, and I take it seriously. I meet my friends there. I also like the principal. She's very gentle and patient, and she has a good heart. She understands me and loves all of us. She helps us solve our problems. I respect my teachers. Even if a teacher wrongs me—which makes me angry—I still respect her. I always like to get the highest grade in the class—perfect scores. When I don't get the highest grade, I get angry. I don't ever remember a time when I took an exam without studying until late at night, even when I was in the first grade.

I like anyone who encourages learning, because learning is important in life, and God and the Prophet ordered us to study. God considers those who seek knowledge to fall into the ranks of the prophets. There is a saying "The teacher was about to be a prophet." Teachers can affect generations to come. We live in an era of continuous innovations.

My favorite school subjects are English and Religion. I read Charles Dickens's novel *Oliver Twist*. It was interesting to read about the way of life in British society. I also like to study Arabic grammar and poetry. Recently, I wrote a story called "*Zeituna and Leimuna*," in English, "The Olive and the Lemon." My cousin and I thought about looking for a producer to make it into a film, but we never did it. We thought no one would support us.

But sometimes school is a burden. Some teachers don't allow us to leave the classroom. They suspect we might be running away from class! But of course this isn't true. It's just that some classes are boring. History class is an example of this. Sometimes what a teacher demands is unreasonable. For example, a teacher may say, "Sit in your place and be

"I like anyone who encourages learning, because learning is important in life, and God and the Prophet ordered us to study."

quiet, you're coming to school for your own good." But I know what's good for me. Also many teachers give us difficult and useless exams. Sometimes we have to take two exams a day. We complain to the principal about this, but nothing happens.

One day a girl brought a newspaper to the classroom. There was an article in it about students' rights. The teacher said, "This is wrong. It's true that students have rights, but they also have duties." We told him. "To be fair, give us our rights, and we'll do our duty."

Once we had a book fair at school. I made miniatures about two stories, one in Arabic (*Uhud battle*) and one in English (*Oliver Twist*). British visitors came to our school to evaluate our English skills. I explained in English about the miniatures. The visitors approved of the level of English in the class and thanked the teacher for her work on the miniatures. The teacher failed to tell them that the miniatures were *our* work. She alone got the praise. After the visitors left, we reminded her that the miniatures were the result of our efforts.

In my school, boys and girls are neither friends nor enemies. It's better for girls to have friends of the same sex because there are things that are special to girls. For example, girls tell each other, "I bought a dress or a skirt or a bracelet." These things just don't interest boys. A boy's mind is on other things, like soccer and TV. I prefer separation between girls and boys, not because we're shy, but because it's more comfortable. The only exchange we have with boys is when we take exams or have an issue with a teacher.

I have three best friends. I love friends with whom I have mutual understanding and loyalty. That's to say, if I tell a friend a secret, she'll keep it. I would reveal someone's secret only if I thought she would get hurt by my not revealing it.

I always feel that I should be of help to others. Recently, I met a woman holding a baby who asked me to go shopping for her. I did it without hesitation. I also help my classmates. And if I see small children fighting, I immediately step in and stop them. I'm a Muslim, and Islam calls for good deeds. Islam teaches me to be kind and helpful to others.

It's a must to solve the conflict between Israelis and Palestinians because otherwise the situation will stay the same forever. If one side attacks, the other will act to take revenge. We want a solution. Stopping the violence would be a victory in itself. One of the two parties should give in to the other. Palestinians are just defending themselves. Peace would serve both parties.

I don't like to listen to the news. It just doesn't please the heart. I don't recommend that sick people listen to the news. It's not good for their health. What we hear daily is just about who is injured, who is murdered, and so on.

It's a pity to spend money on wars. In fact, Israel would be helping itself if it makes peace. Instead of spending money for weapons and tanks, money should be spent for education, medical treatment, and social welfare. The situation now is getting worse in every way. The prime minister and his government collect taxes from people and spend it on weapons— planes and tanks. This is not good, because Israel has many poor people. People say that Israel is rich, but many people are suffering from hunger.

The prime minister is not a just person. I don't say that because I'm an Arab, but because he is, in fact, not just! Even many Jews don't like him. He has to learn to respect Palestinians. I think that the government must be changed.

If peace were to come, everyone would benefit. The Arab world would come to Israel, and Israelis would go to Arab countries. Jews don't go to Ramallah, though it's very beautiful. They also don't go to countries like Syria. With peace, they would feel calm inside. When Jews speak Arabic with me, I'm happy. An Israeli woman, who works with my father, is learning Arabic. Just the way we learn Hebrew, Jews should learn Arabic so that we can communicate better with one another.

My dream is to pass my comprehensive exams and to succeed in my university studies and in all of life. And if I were to become rich, I'd give money to poor people, whether Jews, Christians, or Muslims. But I'd keep part of it for myself to build a house. I'd also travel abroad. I'd try especially hard to establish a peace organization.

My ultimate dream is to unite the world, removing all borders. Most wars occur because the world is divided into countries with borders. I'd cancel the names of all countries. There would be no America, no Israel, no Palestine, no Turkey. There would be just one flag for one world, a "world of peace."

CHAPTER 34

YUVAL

"I've always known that I can come home and tell Mom everything that's on my mind. She's also everybody's mother. When people sleep at my home and wake up in the morning, they say, 'Good morning, Mom.'"

My name is Yuval Rosenberg. I'll be sixteen in August. I'm a student in Rabin High School in Kfar Saba, where I'll be going into the eleventh grade. I live with my mother, brother, and sister.

My mom is the most awesome mother in the whole world. Her name is Galia. One of the things that I value most about our relationship is that I don't hide anything from her. I've always known that I can come home and tell Mom everything that's on my mind. She's also everybody's mother. My friends come to visit me—but also to see her. Before she flew to the United States for Passover last spring, six of my friends came here to say good-bye to her. When people sleep at my home and wake up in the morning, they say, "Good morning, Mom." What makes her so special is that she's an open-minded person. There are many parents who are closed to new ideas. They're stuck in one way of thinking and just can't let go of it.

When I return from school, it's usually lunchtime. Mom prepares the food. It's very pleasant. We sit at the table, and I tell about how the day was and about this and that. She helps me with all kinds of crises in my life. For example, this past year I had a serious problem with my studies. Mom helped me all year long. Finally I was promoted to the eleventh grade with only one failure on my report card. I had had seven failures on earlier report cards. Everything is OK now, thanks to Mom. She just did not let me rest. She sat on me for a month and told me to use this time to improve myself. In fact, the only reason I stay in school is to not disappoint her. I don't see anything that's really positive about school right now. But I know that if I leave, I may regret it later on. That's how I feel.

If I stopped studying now, I would go to work, but I'm not sure what kind of work I'd do. If I leave school and go to work, I'll probably have more time to think about what I want to do with my life. One thing I would like to do is to play the guitar and to start recording some of the songs I play with my friend. We've created some special songs, and we could use our friend's recording studio.

My brother, Asaf, is thirteen. Our relationship is basically very nice.

However, sometimes he'll start annoying me. I smack him when that happens, but I do it lightly. And that situation occurs less frequently now. Sometimes we sit and talk seriously about this and that. There's nothing that I can't tell him, and vice versa.

My patience is often tested by both my siblings. They come to my room to watch TV and continually change channels, looking for something they might like. It's annoying, but I've gotten used to it. As I grow older, I'm becoming a more patient person. I think my "patience genes" come from my mother.

I have a lot of friends. The friend I love best is Nadav. I've only known him since ninth grade, but it seems as if we've known each other for years. We laugh together and talk about everything. He's changed my whole life. Nadav had been in my class at school for three years before I got to know him. We joke about how it was a wasted three years. It's interesting how we met. Nadav came up to me at the end of the ninth grade and said, "Excuse me, do you have a cigarette?" I said, "Yes, but where do you plan to smoke? You know we're in school!" He said, "I'll go into the bathroom." So I said, "Awesome, I'll join you." We went and started talking and that's how we got acquainted. Who would believe that such a relationship could develop in such a short time? Since then we've done lots of things together. Nadav was not supposed to come with me to a music festival I was attending. But suddenly I got a phone call from him. "Yuval," he said, "what's happening?" He then tells me he's coming to the festival after all. At this point I'm totally crying, because he's the person I was missing the most at the festival.

I also have a larger circle of friends in school. Nadav came into this group and immediately connected to everyone. Our group has a special place, just for us—a circular garden that once had a well in it. We do a lot of laughing there. Each of my friends is silly in his own special way. They don't let me be sad. When I'm really depressed, they just don't allow me to stay that way.

And I do get depressed sometimes. For example, there was someone I fell in love with not long ago. I asked her if she wanted to move ahead with our relationship. She said she didn't know, that she needed to think

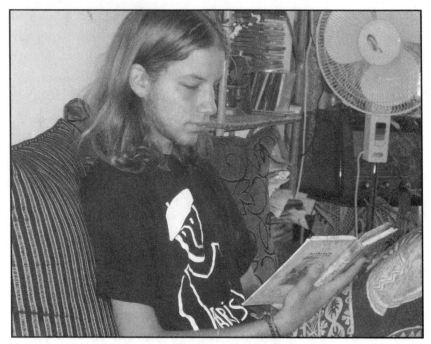

"With regard to our conflict with the Palestinians, it's as if we're the same, and all the time everyone says we're different."

about it. She thought about it for a really long time. That really upset me, and I broke off the relationship, because there's a limit to waiting for love. So right at that tough time my friends came to help me. It happened to be a week when Mom was traveling abroad. My friends came to the house, cooked for me, and made me laugh.

The main thing about celebrating Jewish holidays is being with family and friends and also inviting someone who would not otherwise celebrate these holidays. I have a problem with the Bible. I'm not sure why. I believe there is a God, but I just don't believe in the tradition as it is written in the Bible. I don't believe you need to do such and such. I think there is a superior being who created us the way we are. He will not come and try to make everyone join one particular faith. It's weird when religious people come and try to have people "return" to traditional values.

There's an important question about religion that I think about a lot: If God created us and He is supposedly good, why did He create so many bad people? One answer I thought of is that although God created our world, He can't direct everything. It's the same with our parents. They're also part of a process through which we're created, and they certainly can't control everything. So this is similar to what's happening with God and us.

I don't have any fears about going to the army in two years' time. I believe in fate, that we should let life flow. Whatever happens needs to happen. I have no way of preventing it, so why should I be afraid of it? It's harder for people who believe otherwise. People become traumatized when they think about entering the army. They even try to avoid serving in the army because of their fears.

I have a problem with the settlements. It's complicated. There are people who are being told they have to leave their homes. To take them out of their houses is to remove them from their most secure place. I'm not surprised that they're fighting the orders to leave. If I were told to leave my house, it would be hard, because I've lived here since birth. My house is my foundation. It's my special place. I also have my room here, which is sacred to me. In that room I have my privacy. It's my quiet space. It's the place I know well. I know that it's somewhere I can sit, cry, or be joyful with my friends. Also a place where I can tell my dog secrets—something I love to do, especially considering the fact that she won't reveal them to anyone.

With regard to the conflict with the Palestinians, I think that our people and their people have to arrive at a decision that if there isn't peace, there should at least be a period of truce. Many people say that the Palestinians are to blame for what's happening. Truly, it's not just the Palestinians who are to blame for the situation. There's a wise saying (even though it's childish): "Every fight needs two people." You can't fight solo. The two sides need to arrive at an agreement. It's not just the responsibility of the heads of the government. A whole nation has to arrive at a decision to make peace. Peace has a special meaning for me. It means you can feel really great because you don't need to fight anyone. You don't need to worry.

I started to study Arabic in junior high. Arabic looked more **useful** to me than French, which was my only other choice. To begin with, Palestinians kids often come to Kfar Saba. A few days ago we were in the mall, and some kids started talking to us in Arabic. We didn't understand what they were saying. It shouldn't be that way.

I've met Palestinians my age in the mall. I see them, but I don't have much of a chance to speak with them. I mainly laugh with them when we're together. I go to a youth center where we mainly sit over a cup of coffee and talk about what bothers us. I went there once when Israelis and Palestinians were sitting and talking together. The conversation flowed in lots of directions. It was really nice. It was not about cursing or trying to kill each other. People were calm and relaxed. We sat together, laughed, and listened to the same music. We liked the same computer games. That didn't surprise me. I started to think about such things as what in the world we're really fighting about. It's as if we're the same, and all the time everyone says we're different. Where's the difference?

CONCLUDING NOTES

Teen Voices from the Holy Land: Who Am I to You? was born from the passion of its authors to create a series of books, films, and multimedia presentations that would promote mutual understanding among peoples in conflict anywhere in the world. In this spirit, the authors have founded a nonprofit organization, the Global Oral History Project (GOHIP). The mission of GOHIP is to foster synergistic relationships between cultural groups who regard each other solely through the lenses of their own dominant narratives. Such narratives most often serve to exclude or marginalize the other group. GOHIP encourages peoples in conflict to comprehend the experiences of those on the other side. Such understanding is not merely cognitive in nature. For peoples to live in peace, they must come to know one another with the whole of themselves. This book is a manifestation of GOHIP's mission.

Although a primary audience for this book is young adults, people of all ages can profit from listening to and respecting the narratives of the other.

Through this book we encourage peoples in conflict to tell their histories to one another, harnessing the unique power of the story to fulfill its objectives. Our aim is to promote experiences wherein each cultural group will listen to the life narratives of the other *as they were experienced and as they are understood by that group.* Through this sharing of personal histories, a creative dialogue can emerge, one in which simplistic understandings of the experiences of the other group are replaced by more complex and morally nuanced views. By listening to these narratives, each party to a conflict has the opportunity to see the other side's perspective. Telling and listening to stories can move peoples toward dialogue in ways inaccessible to those who merely engage in discursive argument.

One of the main conflicts on the world stage for nearly a century has been, and continues to be, the Israeli-Palestinian conflict. We firmly believe that a just solution to the ongoing strife in this region will have a positive effect on the welfare of peoples throughout the globe. Strategies employed to resolve the Middle East conflict have generally been based on short-term, often narrowly conceived political calculations. It is critical to pay attention to the long-term goal of helping the peoples of the region learn to live together as neighbors. Rather than focusing on what divides peoples, GOHIP endeavors to portray the interests and hopes that ordinary Palestinians and Israelis share. Rather than giving emphasis to the words and deeds of the region's *leaders*, GOHIP aims to give voice to *those who are led.* We believe that the politics of the region should be viewed as but one of the many dimensions of the lives of its inhabitants. For example, GOHIP has put out a short video celebrating our common human heritage with a collage of wedding ceremonies of the three monotheistic traditions in the Middle East. Those who have viewed the film were in many cases unable to distinguish one ceremony from another.

The aim of this book is to introduce the reader to the peoples who live in the Middle East in a way that is more nuanced and balanced than other accounts. We hope that *Teen Voices from the Holy Land* will foster thoughts about tolerance in the Middle East, in the United States, and throughout the world. We see our work as a counterforce to the mainstream media that all too often reveal a distinct bias. Ideology rules the day in most mainstream media depictions of the politics and other facets of life in the region. Unlike these accounts, our book lets the children of the Middle East speak for themselves. They are invited to express the full range of thoughts and emotions regarding many aspects of their day-to-day lives. What we derive from these stories is the opposite of that which comes filtered through the ideological lenses of the mass media.

It is of special importance to present a nuanced account of life in the Middle East through the medium of the *written* word. We wish to fill what we perceive to be a void in this medium's endeavor to depict life in the Middle East. Even those few published works that attempt to give voice to the children of the region usually fail to move beyond the narrowly political to embrace a more comprehensive range of a child's experiences. While a nearly century-old conflict serves as the context in which each child speaks, we believe that *Teen Voices from the Holy Land* taps into that common well of humanity that gives hope for the future of this region, as well as for the world at large.

An in-depth examination of the teenagers' accounts in this book reveals several key insights that call for further consideration. Looking again at the categories around which we organized our interviews, we can see that the teenagers have alerted us to what we, as educators, believe are vital issues in the areas of family and neighborhood dynamics, community infrastructure, schooling, religion, and politics. The issues raised here are interdependent: a change in one affects them all. We believe that the education systems in both the Israeli and the Palestinian communities must pay special attention to these issues if a genuine and lasting peaceful solution to the conflict in the region is to be achieved. Further, we believe that the principles that lie at the core of these issues must be addressed anywhere and everywhere in the world where conflict reigns.

FAMILY AND NEIGHBORHOOD DYNAMICS

The importance of close family ties is emphasized by both Israeli and Palestinian teens. Despite identifying some areas of disagreement, teenagers from both communities speak repeatedly of their love and respect for their parents. Further, Palestinian and Israeli children alike speak of the importance of communal ties within their neighborhoods and towns. We believe that leaders in the region may well learn to build on family and neighborhood ties as they seek to bridge gaps between the parties to conflict in the Middle East. Respect and affection for those living *within* a family or neighborhood must be nurtured if a generation of young people is to become capable of showing respect and affection for those living *outside* family and community structures. Strong families and communities are critical for the creation of a healthy society, one that is prepared to understand the needs of others.

COMMUNITY INFRASTRUCTURE

It is apparent from the Palestinian teenagers' narratives that their communities within the Green Line suffer from a pronounced lack of resources, such as modern sports facilities. Many children cannot begin to realize their dreams for the future in the absence of a community infrastructure that would support such dreams. Often those who wish to seriously engage in such ordinary pursuits as basketball or swimming do not find those resources in their local communities.

Some Palestinian children indicate that they do not dare to dream at all. And many feel that they constitute a minority whose interests are not honored by a Jewish majority that enjoys privileged status within Israel. The children describe access to sport facilities and clubhouses for Palestinians as severely limited. This disparity with regard to resources is alarming. It fuels frustration, anger, and feelings of worthlessness among numerous Palestinian teenagers. Some of this anger is directed toward the local leadership in Palestinian towns. Many Palestinian children speak of local corruption and the misuse by Palestinian leaders of the few resources that do exist. However, most of the frustration and anger is directed toward the policies of the Israeli government. We believe it is important for the government of Israel to attend to these concerns if there is to be a just resolution of this conflict.

SCHOOLING

Although both Israeli and Palestinian teenagers have positive experiences with their teachers and schools, many complain that their teachers care very little about students' welfare. Several children feel that their teachers lack a commitment to educate effectively. If young people, who are the hope for a peaceful future, are to grow and prosper, educators at all levels must commit themselves to a passionate embrace of their vocation.

We do not have a simple explanation for why some of the teachers mentioned show a lack of care for their students. Nor do we claim to have an easy remedy for it. In these cultures, as in many others, some teachers lose their passion for their vocation. It is evident to us that faculty development initiatives, including ongoing workshops and sabbatical leaves, must be increased in both Israeli and Palestinian schools in order to reinvigorate teachers. If they are to provide guidance for those who will someday determine the quality of life in this embattled region, teachers must themselves embark on the path of active learning.

If education is to provide a central role in preparing the young to become both informed citizens in a democratic society and agents for promoting conflict resolution, *equal* educational opportunities must be offered to both peoples. Inequality of educational opportunity is noted by many Palestinian teenagers. Palestinian students complain of a lack of diverse classroom offerings as well as a lack of both curricular and extracurricular resources. For example, some Palestinian interviewees note that they must leave their local communities and travel to Jewish Israeli schools in order to study certain subjects. Conflict resolution cannot be achieved in the presence of unequal educational opportunities.

The government of Israel has invested more resources in the educational infrastructure of the Jewish community than it has in the school systems of Christian and Muslim communities both in Israel and in the Occupied Territories. As an occupying power—at least between 1967 and 1993—Israel was responsible, under international law, to provide for the welfare of the inhabitants of Palestinian territories. As of this writing, two generations of teenagers have grown up under Occupation. It should be noted that the failure to provide adequate educational resources for Palestinian junior high and high school students continued even after the Palestinian National Authority assumed partial control of Palestinian schools in the Territories in 1993.

This failure on the part of the Israeli government to provide adequate educational resources for Palestinian teenage students is but one example of an underlying and fundamental inequality in other areas of the day-to-day lives of Israelis and Palestinians. As many Palestinian teens indicate in their narratives, an asymmetry exists between the two parties to the conflict: Palestinians living within the Green Line suffer from a failure on the part of the Israeli government to grant them full citizenship rights. And Palestinians living in the Territories experience the everyday consequences of living under Occupation. The teenagers' accounts give ample reason for us to believe that a just resolution of the conflict will not be achieved until the Occupation ends and full rights are given to Palestinians holding Israeli citizenship.

RELIGION

The teens we interviewed held diverse views regarding their religious beliefs. For some, following the basic principles of their religious tradition was said to be of vital importance. Some others held only perfunctory attitudes toward their religion. For a few, questioning God's justice was more important than debating questions of God's existence or understanding the exact nature of ritual observance. Most children spoke of religion largely in terms of an attachment to the traditional ways of their culture. Many were concerned with whether or not they had followed the letter of their religion's laws. Very few spoke of religion as a central force leading them to actively pursue just solutions to the conflict raging around them.

Religion continues to be understood by the media as a major divisive force in the region. And many political leaders view the conflict primarily through ethnic and religious lenses. The teenagers in this book, however, do not seem to understand the conflict as one principally fueled by religious passions. They see the conflict as a dispute over land, with economic and social concerns foremost in their minds. The testimonies of these teenagers give the reader hope that without religious or ethnic passions fanning the flames of hatred, land and resources may be shared in an equitable manner.

POLITICS AND THE CONFLICT

Most of the children interviewed express the desire to share land. Peaceful coexistence is a clearly stated goal. For all of the teens, knowing "the other" is essential if there is to be a just resolution of the conflict. Nearly every child cites the importance of engaging in meaningful dialogue with the other side. There is no doubt that these young people, and others like them, are the hope for a peaceful future in the region. Several Palestinian and Israeli interviewees have come to realize the importance of the role they will play in the future. They speak about the need to move beyond the inactivity of their leaders and they express their desire to take such responsibility upon themselves. All Palestinian and Israeli children need to be encouraged to take responsibility on a grassroots level for working toward a just resolution of differences.

If so many teenagers are desirous of dialogue, why is such dialogue, for the most part, *not* occurring? One plausible answer resides in the fact that political leaders have failed to provide forums that encourage and support dialogue. On the contrary, the rhetoric of politicians (and of mainstream media) tends to emphasize exclusion or separation, rather than inclusion.

Most Palestinian children express, in one form or another, the belief that Israelis do not care to know who they are. They assert that Israelis see them as unworthy, as people belonging to a community that lacks the desire to progress. These Palestinian teenagers believe that Israelis simply do not want to bother with them. And several of the Israeli teenagers interviewed exhibit a sense of detachment from what is occurring in their own region. Many indicate, in subtle ways, that they are tired of the conflict. Wearied, they just want to go on with their lives, living as normally as possible.

As some of both the Israeli and the Palestinian teens imply, Israel, as the stronger party, must assume the burden of responsibility for initiating and sustaining dialogue with Palestinians. We agree with those Israeli children who contend that Jews, fleeing intolerable oppression, have served to dispossess huge numbers of an indigenous Palestinian people. What may be inferred from several of the teens' testimonies is that Israelis must acknowledge the fact of this dispossession as they proceed to work with Palestinian partners toward a just and equitable division of the land. Such an acknowledgment would greatly affect the minds of Palestinians and speak directly to their hearts.

This is not to say that Palestinian leaders are to be absolved of all responsibility for what has occurred and what continues to occur. As several Palestinian teens imply, Palestinian leaders have repeatedly failed to seize opportunities to move toward a just accommodation, often jeopardizing the safety and well-being of their people in the process. However, we conclude along with most of the teens that the Israeli leadership must take those initial steps toward peacemaking that, morally speaking, are demanded of the more powerful party to a conflict.

We believe that addressing these issues that emerge from the thirty-four interviews in this book will help promote a peaceful resolution of the Palestinian-Israeli conflict and will provide hope for those involved in conflict resolution anywhere in the world.

In sum, we believe that the personal stories told spontaneously by these teenagers will contribute to their own recognition of each other's humanity. With the feel of the other's humanity resonating throughout the stories, the teenagers cannot marginalize and ultimately dehumanize one another. These teen voices are the bridge to mutual respect and understanding, without which the foundation for long-term coexistence and peace cannot be realized.

APPENDIX A

MAP OF THE MIDDLE EAST

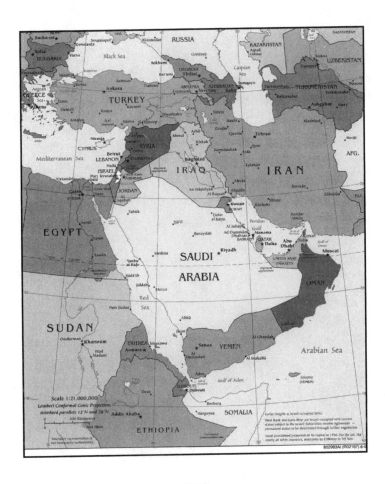

APPENDIX B

MAP OF ISRAEL AND PALESTINE, WITH TEENS' TOWNS

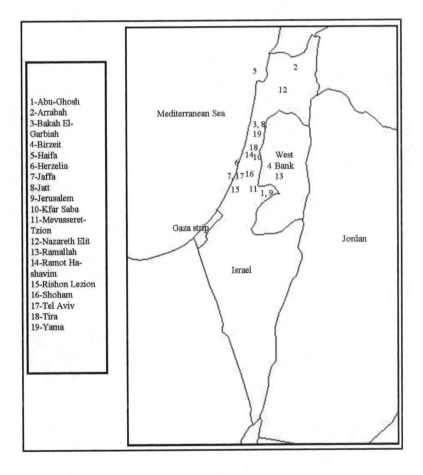

1-Abu-Ghosh
2-Arrabah
3-Bakah El-
Garbiah
4-Birzeit
5-Haifa
6-Herzelia
7-Jaffa
8-Jatt
9-Jerusalem
10-Kfar Saba
11-Mevasseret-
Tzion
12-Nazareth Elit
13-Ramallah
14-Ramot Ha-
shavim
15-Rishon Lezion
16-Shoham
17-Tel Aviv
18-Tira
19-Yama

APPENDIX C

GLOSSARY

Abu-Ghosh. Palestinian town in Israel, eight miles west of Jerusalem. Abu-Ghosh is the home of a Crusader-era monastery.

Al-Aksa. The third-holiest Muslim shrine, a mosque located on the Temple Mount, or Haram-esh-Sharif, in Jerusalem.

Al-Muqata. Arabic for *compound*, used in recent years to refer to the headquarters of (former and now deceased) Palestinian Authority president Yasser Arafat. Al-Muqata is located in Ramallah, a large city on the West Bank that is recognized as the seat of government of the Palestinian Authority.

Al-Muthalath. Arabic for *the triangle*; refers to an area in the northeast of Israel where there are large numbers of Palestinian villages, towns, and cities. Two hundred and fifty thousand residents live in this area, inhabiting towns such as Tira and Jatt.

Al-Sheik Ahmad Yasin. Leader of Muslim resistance movement, assassinated by Israelis in 2004. He was born in 1938 south of the Gaza Strip. He suffered a sports accident as a youth; as a result, his legs and hands became paralyzed. A well-known preacher in the mosques of the Gaza Strip, Yasin established the Islamic Resistance Movement, Hamas, in 1987. In 1989, the Israelis arrested Yasin along with hundreds of Hamas members in an attempt to stop armed resistance.

Allah. Arabic name for the One True God. Most Muslims in the

West use *Allah* and *God* interchangeably. *Allah* is a comprehensive name for the God who has ninety-nine attributes, or descriptive names, such as "the Compassionate" and "the Merciful."

Alterman, Natan. Israeli poet and journalist (1910–1970). Alterman is known for his poems dealing with social and political issues, as well as poems of a more lyrical and meditative nature.

Amir, Yigal. Jewish Israeli extremist who assassinated Israeli prime minister Yitzhak Rabin in 1995. Amir was convicted of the murder and given a life sentence in 1996.

Arrabah. Palestinian village located in the northwestern region of Israel known as the Galilee, northeast of Haifa.

***bagrut* exams.** Examinations in the Israeli education system conducted toward the end of high school to gauge readiness for university studies.

Bakah al Garbiah. Palestinian town in Israel, about thirty miles northeast of Tel Aviv in an area known as "the triangle." Bakah al Garbiah abuts the Green Line and is separated only by the Israeli-established wall from the West Bank town of Bakah al Sharkiya.

bar mitzvah. Literally, "son of commandment." At the age of thirteen (twelve for a girl, who is said to be bat mitzvah, daughter of commandment), Jewish boys participate in a ceremony that ritualizes their obligation to observe biblical commandments and that admits them into the Jewish community.

Barak, Ehud. Israeli prime minister, 1999–2001. Barak led the Israeli side of negotiations with the Palestinians at Camp David in 2000.

Birzeit. Palestinian town, located in the West Bank, about nine miles northeast of Jerusalem. It is the home of Birzeit University, the first university to be established on the West Bank.

Chanukah. Jewish Festival of Lights celebrated for eight days, usually in the month of December. The holiday commemorates the Jewish revolt against Syrian oppressors in the second century before the Common Era.

checkpoints. Places on the Green Line, at the entrance to the Gaza Strip and within the West Bank, where Israeli military authorities check the identity papers of all those passing through. Israel claims that checkpoints are necessary for security purposes. Some Israelis argue that checkpoints create more hostility on the part of Palestinians, thus endangering the same Israelis they are designed to protect. Checkpoints often delay travel by Palestinians for many hours, sometimes endangering the lives of the sick and the vulnerable.

dabka. Arabic line dance, often performed at joyous gatherings, such as weddings. *Dabka* is an important part of Arab life. The dance is performed by men only, women only, or in mixed company. Steps often include rhythmic stomping and hopping.

Dubai. One of the seven emirates that compose the United Arab Emirates, located on the southeastern tip of the Arabian Peninsula.

Eid Al Adha. Feast of Sacrifice, the most important feast of the Muslim calendar. It concludes the Pilgrimage to Mecca and lasts for three days, commemorating Ibrahim's (Abraham's) willingness to obey God by sacrificing his son. Muslims believe the son to be Ismail, considered the forefather of Arab peoples. The feast reenacts Ibrahim's obedience to God by sacrificing a cow or a ram. The family typically eats only a portion of the meal, donating the rest to the poor.

fakusa. Arabic term for a vegetable similar to a cucumber.

Fatimah. Daughter of the Prophet Muhammad.

Galilee. Region in northern Israel. Generally, the area northeast of the city of Haifa is known as the Galilee. Jesus lived most of his life in this region, and the miracles described in the Christian Bible are believed to have taken place here. Today, much of the Galilee is home to large numbers of Palestinian villages and towns.

Gaza Strip. Narrow strip of land under the control of the Palestinian Authority as of August 2005. The Strip is bordered on the west by the Mediterranean Sea, on the north and east by Israel, and on the south by Egypt. It is one of the most densely populated areas on the earth, with about 1.4 million Palestinians in an area of 220 square miles. The Strip's borders were originally those of the armistice lines between Egypt and Israel after 1948, following the end of the British Mandate in the area. Egypt controlled the Strip until the 1967 Six Days' War. In

1993, after agreements between Israel and the Palestinian Authority known as the Oslo Accords, the Strip came under the very limited control of the Palestinian Authority. Israeli settlements (with eighty-five hundred Jewish occupants) continued to exist in Gaza until August 2005. As of this writing, border crossings remain under Israeli control, as do maritime access and airspace. Palestinians claim the Strip as a part of a future Palestinian state.

Green Line. Boundary between Israel and the West Bank and the Gaza Strip. The Green Line is the armistice line drawn at the close of the 1948 Arab-Israeli War. Today it is the internationally recognized demarcation line between Israel and the West Bank and Gaza Strip.

Hadera. City in Israel of about seventy-five thousand inhabitants. Hadera is located between Tel Aviv and Haifa.

Haifa. City in Israel, lying between the Mediterranean Sea and the Carmel Mountain range. Haifa has about three hundred thousand residents, including substantial numbers of Palestinians. It is Israel's major seaport.

Haj. Pilgrimage to Mecca in Hijaz province, Saudi Arabia, the holiest city in Islam. The city is the site where Ibrahim, together with his son Ismail, built the Ka'ba, a rectangular brick building surrounded by the great mosque al-Haram. Making the pilgrimage to Mecca is one of the five "pillars" of Islam. The pilgrimage is required of all Muslims at least once in a lifetime, though there are exceptions for those who are physically unable to make the trek. The Haj is considered "the ultimate act of worship" in Islam.

Herzlia. Israeli city of about one hundred thousand, about eight miles north of Tel Aviv on the Mediterranean Sea. It is a resort as well as a center of the high-tech industry in Israel.

intifada. Arabic for *uprising.* Uprisings protesting the continuing Occupation by Israel of the West Bank and Gaza occurred in the late 1980s and, again, beginning in the year 2000.

Jaffa. Ancient city, located in the southern part of the Tel Aviv–Jaffa municipality. For thousands of years, what is today known as Jaffa was the only city in the region and its most ancient site, having been built in approximately 5000 BCE. It has often served as a target of conquering peoples because of its strategic position at the crossroads of Europe, Africa, and Asia. Until the twentieth century, visitors to Palestine entered through Jaffa. Jaffa today has about eighty thousand inhabitants. Most Palestinian inhabitants live in the older part of the city.

Jatt. Palestinian town in Israel, approximately thirty miles northeast of Tel Aviv. Jatt, a city of eight thousand, exists adjacent to the site of an ancient mound about six thousand years old. The town is home to large numbers of teachers and other professionals.

Jerusalem. Two-thousand-year-old city situated on a hilltop thirty-five miles east of the Mediterranean Sea. Jerusalem is the home of the world's three monotheistic religions: Judaism, Christianity, and Islam. It contains sites deemed holy to all three traditions. Between 1948 and 1967, Jerusalem was formally divided into an eastern sector (inhabited almost entirely by Christian and Muslim Palestinians and controlled by Jordan) and a western sector, inhabited almost entirely by Jewish Israelis and named the capital of modern-day Israel. As a result of the Six Days' War, East Jerusalem fell into the hands of Israel. Palestinians consider Jerusalem to be the capital of a future Palestinian state.

Kalthum, Um. Egyptian popular singer of the 1960s and 1970s, credited with shaping much of contemporary Arabic music. She is especially noted for her lengthy songs.

Kfar Saba. Israeli city of over eighty thousand inhabitants, located about twelve miles northeast of Tel Aviv.

kibbutz. Israeli collective community. The kibbutz is owned by its members, who make joint decisions about the welfare of the community. For most of the twentieth century, kibbutzim were predominantly agricultural. In more recent years, industry has played an increasingly dominant role in the economics of the kibbutz.

kiddush. Hebrew prayer over wine, recited on the Sabbath and other major Jewish holidays. Those who recite the kiddush bless God's name, inaugurating a holy time and thanking God for creating "the fruit of the vine."

Labor Movement. All of the governments of Israel until 1977 were oriented toward the social democratic values of the Labor Party. Currently, the Labor Party is the second-largest political party in Israel.

Land of Israel. Term used by many right-wing Israelis to refer to land allegedly belonging to Jews by virtue of what is written in the Hebrew Bible. It connotes borders that are substantially larger than those of the State of Israel.

Maaleh Hahamisha. Kibbutz, or collective community, located six miles northwest of Jerusalem.

Maccabi. Hebrew name (referring to an ancient warrior family) given to sports clubs and associations in Israel.

Memorial Garden. Garden in the city of Kfar Saba, northeast of Tel Aviv, commemorating those killed during the ongoing conflict with Palestinians.

Mevasseret-Tzion. Bedroom suburb, five miles west of Jerusalem. Established by Moroccan and Kurdish Jews in the 1950s, the town now has a population of more than twenty-five thousand.

Middle East. Loosely defined geographical region encompassing the mainly Arab states east of the Mediterranean, as well as Turkey, and, sometimes, the nations along the northern rim of the African continent. The Middle East is often referred to as the "cradle of civilization." In recent times, the region, comprising the meeting place of three continents, has been the source of fierce struggles and continuous political turmoil, including the Israeli-Palestinian conflict.

muezzin. Muslim crier who calls the faithful to prayer five times a day. A muezzin is chosen on the basis of good voice and good character. When calling Muslims to prayer, the muezzin faces each of the four directions in turn.

mulukhiyah. Leafy summer vegetable, popular among Palestinians and other peoples of the Middle East.

Nazareth Elit. Hebrew for "Upper Nazareth," a city overlooking the Palestinian city of Nazareth in the Lower Galilee, twenty-five miles east of Haifa. The city has more than fifty thousand inhabitants, almost all of them Jewish. Nazareth is the largest Palestinian city in Israel. It is also the birthplace of Jesus.

Occupation. Generally understood under international law as the exercise by one power of control over territory not within the recognized sovereignty of that power without the consent of the population of the territory. With regard to the Israeli-Palestinian conflict, the term refers to Israeli control of the West Bank and Gaza Strip, an area deemed by the international community as belonging to the Palestinian people.

ORT. Refers to a worldwide network of secondary schools focusing on job training.

Oslo Accords. Agreement forged in 1993 between Israel and the Palestinians. Israel recognized the PLO (see following entry), granting limited autonomy in the West Bank and Gaza. The PLO agreed to end Intifada. The Palestinian National Authority was established two years later.

PLO. Palestine Liberation Organization. Political movement, created in 1964, uniting Palestinians in an effort to create an independent state of Palestine.

Peace Now. Grassroots left-wing political movement in Israel working for a two-state solution of the Israeli-Palestinian conflict on the basis of the principle of "land for peace."

Quran. Holy Book of Islam, revealed to the Prophet Muhammad by Allah in the cities of Mecca and Medina. The period of revelation is thought to be between 610 and 632. The Quran is divided into 114 chapters or suras. The meaning of *Quran* is thought to be connected either to the word for "tie together" or the word for "recite." The Quran is regarded as the sound of Islam. When recited according to a sacred rhythm, a holy atmosphere is created.

Rabin, Yitzhak. Prime minister of Israel from 1974 to 1977 and 1992 to 1995. Rabin was a supporter of the Oslo Accords. He was assassinated in 1995 by right-wing ideologue Yigal Amir.

Rahbat Mar Yusif Tawjih. Palestinian high school in Ramallah.

Ramadan. Ninth month of the lunar calendar. During this month, Muslims observe a fast during daylight hours. In the evening, meals are shared with family and friends. It is a time of worship and contemplation, as well as a time for reinforcing family and community ties.

Ramallah. Palestinian city a few miles northeast of Jerusalem on the West Bank. Ramallah is the government seat of the Palestinian Authority, including most of its legislative and executive offices. It has over sixty thousand residents.

Ramat Gan. Israeli city bordering Tel Aviv on the east, with over one hundred and thirty thousand inhabitants. It is the home of Bar Ilan University.

Ras-El-Amud. Neighborhood of East Jerusalem overlooking the Old City, the site of holy places in Jerusalem.

Rishon LeZion. Israeli city south of Tel Aviv, founded in 1882 by Russian immigrants. Rishon LeZion has become one of Israel's main centers of wine making.

roadblocks. Rubble-laden barriers on roads within the Occupied Territories. The Israeli army places these barriers as security measures to prevent free access by Palestinians.

security wall or security fence. Combination of electrified fence and cement wall that, when completed by the Israeli military, will stretch for more than four hundred miles. Guard towers, motion detectors, and trenches are also part of what Israel refers to as a "security wall," whose stated purpose is to prevent incursions by Palestinians. The wall is built in part along the Green Line, but it snakes around several major settlements, incorporating substantial sections of the West Bank. The wall divides the West Bank into distinct small areas, splitting some existing Palestinian communities, rendering impossible the existence of other cohesive communities, and making travel between Palestinian cities, towns, and villages difficult or impossible.

seder. Ritual meal served during the Passover holiday to commemorate the liberation of Jewish slaves from Egypt in ancient times. The story of the Exodus from Egypt is read.

settlements. Jewish Israeli population centers on land deemed by international law as occupied. These settlements in the West Bank, currently numbering over one hundred, were established by successive

Israeli governments following the Six Days' War. As of this writing, some two hundred and fifty thousand Jewish Israelis live in these settlements. If the Jewish residents of East Jerusalem are included in the count, the number reaches more than four hundred and fifty thousand. Bypass roads, for Jewish use only, have been established to link the settlements to one another and to the major access points within Israel. Many Israelis are opposed to the settlements; others see them as bolstering Israeli security; still others wish to have the land on which settlers live become part of "Greater Israel." Others remain neutral. Some Israelis and all Palestinians believe that settlements impede, or render impossible, movement toward the creation of a viable Palestinian state on the West Bank and Gaza.

Sharm al-Sheikh. Egyptian city at the tip of the Sinai Peninsula on the Red Sea.

Sharon, Ariel. Elected prime minister of Israel in 2001; reelected in 2003. As of this writing, August 2006, Sharon lies in a coma and has been replaced as prime minister by Ehud Olmert.

Sheikh Jarah. Palestinian neighborhood in East Jerusalem, often known for its international flavor.

Shimshit. Israeli town founded in the 1990s on the southern slopes of the lower Galilee Mountains.

Shoham. Town in Israel, located near Ben Gurion airport, east of Tel Aviv. Shoham was founded in the 1990s and has a population of over twenty thousand.

shokran. Arabic for *thank you.*

Solelim. Israeli kibbutz, or collective farm, located in the lower Galilee.

suicide bombings. Attacks on members of the Israeli military and civilians during which bombers explode a device that kills them and often those in proximity. Many Palestinians disagree with the use of suicide bombings as a mode of resisting Occupation.

Taibeh. Palestinian town in Israel, approximately eighteen miles northeast of Tel Aviv and home to over thirty thousand Palestinians.

Territories (Occupied). The West Bank and the Gaza Strip, areas occupied by Israel following the Six Days' War. The Gaza Strip was returned to Palestinian control in 2005, although borders, airspace, and the waters of the Mediterranean adjoining Gaza remain, as of this writing, under Israeli control.

Tira. Palestinian town in Israel, approximately fifteen miles northeast of Tel Aviv, and home to over twenty thousand Palestinians.

Torah. Holy Scriptures in Judaism. The word (which derives from the Hebrew word for *instruction*) can refer to the Five Books of Moses alone, to the entire Hebrew Bible, including the Prophets and Writings, or to the entire body of Jewish law and teachings, including the Talmud, or commentaries on the Bible.

Uhud Battle. Major battle fought between the Prophet Muhammad and his followers and the Meccans around the years 625 through 628.

Wahat el Salaam. Cooperative village and school established by Jewish, Christian, and Muslim citizens of Israel, located halfway between Jerusalem and Tel Aviv. The word means "Oasis of Peace." The village engages in educational work for peace, equality, and mutual understanding between Israelis and Palestinians.

West Bank. Area west of the Jordan River that comprises the 22 percent of historic Palestine that is recognized by the international community as constituting (along with the Gaza Strip) present-day Palestine.

Yama. Town in the "triangle" region of Israel, about thirty miles northeast of Tel Aviv.

Yfaat. Kibbutz, or collective settlement, in the northeastern part of Israel.

Yom Kippur. Jewish Day of Atonement, the holiest time of the Hebrew calendar. Yom Kippur is a day of fasting. Jews pray for forgiveness for sins committed against God. Sins committed against fellow humans cannot be forgiven by God; they must be acknowledged before the human who has been wronged.

TIMELINE OF RECENT PALESTINIAN–ISRAELI HISTORY

1517–1918. Ottoman Empire rules historic Palestine.

1882. Arrival of first wave of European Jewish immigrants, to be followed by successive waves under the influence of the Zionist movement.

1917. Britain issues Balfour Declaration, promising a "National Home" for the Jews in Palestine.

1922. As a result of the defeat of the Ottoman Empire in World War I, Britain is granted mandate in historic Palestine by League of Nations.

1929 and 1936–1939. Violent clashes, as indigenous Palestinian population resists growing Jewish settlements.

1947. UN recommends partition of British-Mandate Palestine into two separate states. Deeming the proposal unjust for its failure to take into account the demographic distribution of Jews and Arabs in the area, Palestinians reject partition plan.

1948–1949. Zionist leaders proclaim State of Israel. Fighting breaks out between Israel and its Arab neighbors. The resulting war is considered by Israel its "War of Independence." Palestinians understand it as al-Nakbah, or "the Catastrophe." Seven hundred and fifty thousand Palestinians are expelled or flee. Armistice agreements are signed between Israel and Egypt, Lebanon, and Syria.

1964. PLO (Palestine Liberation Organization) is founded.

1967. Six Days' War. Israel conducts what it considers a preemptive war against Egypt and, in the ensuing battles with all the Arab states on its borders, occupies the Sinai Peninsula, East Jerusalem, Gaza Strip, the West Bank, and Golan Heights. Israel begins establishing settlements in conquered territories. Palestinians and much of the world community see this settlement activity as a violation of international law. United Nations Resolution 242 calls for Israeli withdrawal from Occupied Territories.

1973. Yom Kippur War (October War). Egypt retakes the Suez Canal and a narrow zone on its other side in a surprise attack. Backed by US supplies of arms, Israel succeeds in pushing back the Syrians and Egyptians.

1979. Peace treaty is signed between Egypt and Israel, brokered by President Jimmy Carter in Camp David. Israel returns the Sinai Peninsula to Egypt in return for peace and normalizing of relations.

1982. Israel invades Lebanon to establish security zone in order to prevent attacks on northern Israeli communities and to expel the PLO from Lebanon. Israel remains in Lebanon until its withdrawal from all but the security zone in south Lebanon in 1985.

1982. Palestinian residents of Sabra and Shatila refugee camps in Lebanon are murdered by Israeli-allied Christian militias under Israel's watch.

1987. First Intifada (uprising) begins in Gaza Strip and West Bank. Palestinians, armed with rocks, continue fighting against the Occupation until 1993. More than twenty thousand are killed or wounded, almost all Palestinians.

1988. Jordan renounces all claims to the West Bank. Palestinians accept UN Resolution 242 and call for Palestinian state alongside Israel.

1991. Madrid Peace Conference.

1993. Following secret talks, the Oslo Declaration of Principles is announced. Israel recognizes the PLO, granting it limited autonomy in the West Bank and Gaza. The PLO agrees to end Intifada. The Palestinian Authority is established two years later.

1995. Israeli prime minister Yitzhak Rabin is assassinated by Yigal Amir, a right-wing Israeli extremist.

2000. In the face of the stalled progress of Oslo commitments, President Clinton calls for Chairman Yasser Arafat and Prime Minister Ehud Barak to meet at Camp David. The summit fails, each side accusing the other of taking uncompromising positions.

2000. Second (Al-Aksa) Intifada breaks out following the Israeli opposition leader Ariel Sharon to the Temple Mour both Jews and Muslims.

2001. Right-wing Likud leader Ariel Sharon is elec ister in Israel, replacing Ehud Barak.

2002. Israel reoccupies all major Palestinian Israel begins building security wall/fence in th

2002. Saudi peace initiative is adopted at an Arab League summit, promising peace in return for Israel's return to 1967 borders.

2004. International court of justice rules that the Israeli security wall is in violation of international law and should be torn down.

2004. Yasser Arafat dies.

2005. Mahmoud Abbas is elected president of the Palestinian National Authority.

2005. Israel evacuates all settlements in Gaza Strip.

2006. Prime Minister Ariel Sharon suffers stroke and lapses into coma. He is replaced as prime minister by Ehud Olmert.

2006. Legislative elections are held by Palestinians. Hamas emerges as winner.

2006. Thirty-four-day war between Israel and Lebanon.

APPENDIX E

RECOMMENDED READINGS (SELECTED)

Buber, Martin. *A Land of Two Peoples*, edited by Paul Mendes-Flohr. Gloucester, MA: Peter Smith, 1994.

Farsoun, Samih K. *Palestine and the Palestinians*. Boulder, CO: Westview, 2000.

Khalidi, Rashid. *Palestinian Identity: The Construction of Modern National Consciousness*. New York: Columbia University Press, 1997.

Laqueur, Walter, and Rubin Barry, eds. *The Israel-Arab Reader: A Documentary History of the Middle East Conflict*. New York: Penguin Group, 2001.

Lerner, Michael. *Healing Israel/Palestine: A Path to Peace and Reconciliation*. New York: Tikkun Books, 2003.

Morris, Benny. *Righteous Victims: A History of the Zionist/Arab Conflict, 1881–2001*. New York: Vintage Books, 2001.

Said, Edward. *The End of the Peace Process: Oslo and After*. New York: Vintage Books, 2001.

———. *The Question of Palestine*. New York: Vintage Books, 1992.